YoungWriters 2006 Poetry Competition

"I have a dream
children will one
where they will r
color of their sk
of their characte

Martin Luther King

I have a dream

words to change the world

* MOTIVATE your pupils to write and appreciate poetry.
* INSPIRE them to share their hopes and dreams for the future.
* BOOST awareness of your school's creative ability.
* WORK alongside the National Curriculum or the
  high level National Qualification Skills.
* Supports the *Every Child Matters - Make a Positive Contribution* outcome.
* Over £7,000 of great prizes for schools and pupils.

"When I was out there I was never ever
alone, there was always a team of people
behind me, in mind if not in body."
Ellen MacArthur

North West England Vol II
Edited by Heather Killingray

 Young**Writers**

First published in Great Britain in 2006 by:
Young Writers
Remus House
Coltsfoot Drive
Peterborough
PE2 9JX
Telephone: 01733 890066
Website: www.youngwriters.co.uk

SB ISBN 1 84602 644 X

Foreword

Imagine a teenager's brain; a fertile yet fragile expanse teeming with ideas, aspirations, questions and emotions. Imagine a classroom full of racing minds, scratching pens writing an endless stream of ideas and thoughts . . .

. . . Imagine your words in print reaching a wider audience. Imagine that maybe, just maybe, your words can make a difference. Strike a chord. Touch a life. Change the world. Imagine no more . . .

'I Have a Dream' is a series of poetry collections written by 11 to 18-year-olds from schools and colleges across the UK and overseas. Pupils were invited to send us their poems using the theme 'I Have a Dream'. Selected entries range from dreams they've experienced to childhood fantasies of stardom and wealth, through inspirational poems of their dreams for a better future and of people who have influenced and inspired their lives.

The series is a snapshot of who and what inspires, influences and enthuses young adults of today. It shows an insight into their hopes, dreams and aspirations of the future and displays how their dreams are an escape from the pressures of today's modern life. Young Writers are proud to present this anthology, which is truly inspired and sure to be an inspiration to all who read it.

Contents

Baines School, Poulton-le-Fylde

Cansfield High School, Wigan

Coppenhall High School, Crewe

Gateacre Community Comprehensive School, Liverpool

Dean Norbury (14)	45
Lauren Donnelly (14)	45
Ellis Williams (14)	46
Hannah Finnigan (14)	46
Nataleigh Williamson (14)	47
Louis Maddison (14)	47
Conner Jones (13)	48
Zoe Lawson (13)	49
Laura Spruce (14)	50

Lostock Hall Community High School, Preston

Jonathan Barton (12)	50
Jayne Threlfall (12)	51
Samuel Caunce (13)	52
Rachel Smith (12)	53
Alice Corrigan (11)	54
Matthew Carr (12)	55
Samantha Curry (11)	56
Rebecca Gidley (12)	57
Natasha Thorpe (12)	58
Robyn Davidson (12)	58
Katrina Embleton (14)	59
Hannah Russell (12)	60
Harry Ryding (12)	61
Aimeé-Jai Dunlop (13)	62
Jake Warburton (12)	62
Sarah Fisher (15)	63
Leanne Martland (15)	63
Jordan Hall (12)	64
Craig Young (14)	64
Katie Blacklidge (12)	65
Antony Hollinghurst (12)	66
Alexandra Jackson (12)	67
Joanne Dixon (15)	68
Bethany Ashworth (11)	69
Darren Wiggans (13)	70
Matthew Waters (13)	71
Liam Osborn (13)	72
Lisa Taylor (13)	72
Jodie Renshaw (13)	73
Matthew Evans (13)	74

Hollie McCarthy (12)   75
Ellis Duncan (12)   76
Daniel Coyne (13)   77

Montgomery High School, Blackpool
Natasha Carney (11)   77
Katy Melling (11)   78
Sam Hodgson (12)   78
Katie Dennett (12)   79
Jake Macrae (12)   79
Ryan Hemming (12)   80
Lloyd Stevenson (11)   80
Charlotte Raby (12)   81
Rebecca Sheehan (12)   82
Emma Wainwright (12)   83
Ashleigh Good (12)   84
Shannon Rees (12)   85
Holly Wadeson (12)   86
Aidan Radcliffe (12)   87
Joshua Barrow (12)   88
Jack McFarlane (12)   88
Becky Hoddinott (12)   89
Louise Latham (12)   89
Hollie Rigby (12)   90
Naomi Gilby (12)   90
Rebecca Davies (12)   91
Rebecca Mills (11)   92
Catherine Pullen (12)   93
Luke Cable (12)   94
Chenice Kiernan (12)   94
Laura Walmsley (12)   95
Thomas Roy Hornsby (12)   95
Louis Garrick (12)   96
Rachel Bullock (12)   97
Bethany Spooner (12)   98
Stephanie Rawlinson (12)   99
Ellie May Austin (12)   100
Lauren Oatley (12)   101
Emma Pilkington (12)   102
William Hirst (12)   103
Jordan Grenaghan (12)   104

Summerseat Residential School, Bury

Corey Leon Jolliffe (13)	131
Adrian Kirkwilliam (15)	132
Antony Mahon (13)	132
Simon Smith (15)	133
Mike Whitnall (15)	134
Lisa Bland (14)	134
Daniel Bates (16)	135
Ashli Charnock (15)	135
Tom Weatherilt (15)	136
Ben Holmes (13)	136
Brendan Cawley (13)	137
Matthew Luttrell (14)	137
Gerry Conneely (15)	138
Ryan Harrison (13)	138
Adam Cooper (15)	139
Reece Bell (13)	139
Luke Percival (14)	140

Upton-by-Chester High School, Chester

Alex Steeland (14)	140
Katie Greenwood (11)	141
James Kellacher (12)	141
Adam Bradley (12)	142
Cara Bebbington (12)	142
Charlotte Jones (12)	143
Sarah Howard (14)	143
Harriet Thatcher (12)	144
Chelsea Woolley (14)	144
John Thompson (14)	145
Ceri Grube (14)	145
Frances Grindley (14)	146
Natasha Price (15)	147
Luke Cowieson (14)	148
Rebecca Brierley (15)	149
Ceri Jones (14)	150
Samantha Carter (15)	151
Matthew Owen (14)	152
Rachael Langan (14)	152
Miriam Peers (12)	153
Jenny Hughes (13)	154

The Poems

Martin Luther King

'I have a dream . . .' that famous phrase
That changed the world in many ways

Two people from a different race
Could not be together in the same place
When applying to schools, people were not let in
Merely because of the colour of their skin
They couldn't even walk on the same side of the street
Changing all this, seemed an impossible feat
But one person, he did change everything
And his name: Martin Luther King
Every day he witnessed discrimination
But didn't walk on by, like the rest of the nation
Instead, he made a stand about what he saw
Even though doing so, he was breaking the law
Although he was shot and later he died
By those words he spoke, we still abide
He is a man known throughout the nation
As a truly great inspiration.

Caroline Green (13)
Baines School, Poulton-le-Fylde

Ronaldinho

He was born to be the best
As a kid, he passed the test
He has the heart of the game
Showing that fouling is to shame
Using tricks, skill never stopping the flow
Now on adverts called Joga Bonito
All he has is friends and mates
He is full of respect, there is no hate
He inspires his teammates and Brazil
With a vital strike and fatal skill
Ronaldinho, player of the years
The player everyone cheers!

Daniel Hopwood (13)
Baines School, Poulton-le-Fylde

This Is What I Want To Be

I want to be a star
And have a really posh car
And have a pool
And be really cool
This is what I want to be.

I want to be a model
I think it will be a doddle
Have gorgeous hair
And act like I don't care
This is what I want to be.

This is what I want to be
I want to be a star
And also a model
Have a posh car
I think it will be a doddle.

Lucy McKenna (12)
Baines School, Poulton-le-Fylde

Mother Teresa

Most of her life was dedicated to caring
What little she had she didn't mind sharing
She helped those in need
With many good deeds.

She was thoughtful and kind
With an intelligent mind
Caring for the sick and poor
She was horrified by what she saw.

During the time she was ill
She carried on still
She was loved worldwide
It was our loss when she died.

Natalie Wright (12)
Baines School, Poulton-le-Fylde

Live Strong

He fought through it all the way,
Each long and dreaded passing day.
He was determined to win this fight,
He wasn't going to give up and die in the night.

He won his races with joy and pride,
But if he lost he knew he'd tried.
He was supported by family and friends,
And he will be until his life ends.

He raised money by creating wristbands,
Then he sold them for a £1 all over the lands.
On his bands he wrote 'live strong',
Good advice, he wasn't wrong.

Now he's retired and cycles no more,
He doesn't do the France cycling tour.
He's settling down with his family,
An inspiration to you and he's an inspiration to me.

Hannah Williams (12)
Baines School, Poulton-le-Fylde

David Beckham

He lives in a nice house in Spain,
He even has his own private plane,
He plays football for Real Madrid,
He's been playing since he was a kid.

He started at United and made the first team,
But to captain England was his ultimate dream,
His drive and determination, he shows in his game,
Has inspired young children to do just the same.

His hard work and dedication,
Has pleased people across the nation,
I have a dream that one day,
Like David Beckham, I could play.

Joanna Hernen (12)
Baines School, Poulton-le-Fylde

I Have A Dream
And What A Dream It Is

I dream of fame,
I dream of glory,
I dream of honour,
I dream of triumph.

It's a dream we all have,
A dream of success,
A dream of hope,
Hope for success.

But the success of hope is not final,
For the success of hope is the beginning,
The beginning of a journey,
A journey of life.

A life inspired,
Inspired by fame,
Inspired by glory,
Inspired by honour,
Inspired by triumph,
Inspired by inspiration itself,
Inspiration inspired by a dream
And what a dream it is.

Thomas Baran (13)
Baines School, Poulton-le-Fylde

I Have A Dream: Dame Kelly Holmes

Bang! goes the gun
The competitors start to run
Here comes England's golden girl
On the ice rink she can twirl

It's home for Holmes
Here she comes
Three cheers, hip hip hooray
Once again she saves the day.

Sarah Stead (13)
Baines School, Poulton-le-Fylde

Tiger Woods

I want to hear the *swoosh* when I swing
Hear the *ping* when I hit the ball
Hear the cheer when I put on the green jacket
I want to be just like Tiger Woods
Hear the *plunk* when I have putted the ball
Wear the Nike tick with pride
See my face in all golf magazines
I want to be just like Tiger Woods
I want to be a threat to all golfers
I want to win the men's British Open
I want to hear the cheer when I have putted an eagle
I want to be just like Tiger Woods
Some people say he is the master of golf
People say he is the best at it
I say he is my hero
I want to be just like Tiger Woods.

Jacob Knapman (13)
Baines School, Poulton-le-Fylde

Truly Inspirational

The doctor who delivered me
Helped my mum in her time of need
Showed compassion and care
Gave his all to alleviate suffering
And out into the world I come
Healthy, happy, safe and wanted.

The nurses who gave my mum a rest
After the birth when she needed it most
They were so gentle, saw to all my needs
Then returned me to the most warm embrace.

As I grew older, with minor complaints,
Toothache, stomach pains, rashes and fevers
Growing pains, cuts and infections
Doctors and nurses saw me through
With diagnosis, medication and dedication.

Ben Agar (13)
Baines School, Poulton-le-Fylde

Steve Gerrard

When you came onto the football scene,
Your lunging tackles were respectfully mean,
Your football ability shook the Earth,
You were a true Red from the day of your birth.

When you walk out of the changing room,
The fans are chanting your tune,
People expect you to control the game,
You are their god, people worship your name.

Respected by all who see,
He has amazing ability,
He passes the ball with his right shoe,
He is a scorer through and through.

His presence is known by all,
He is inspirational to them all,
He is the best from his generation,
He is loved by all the nation.

He is my role model, for not just me,
He is loved by so many,
He isn't like all the rest,
He is better than the best!

Ben Whetton (13)
Baines School, Poulton-le-Fylde

My Dad

My dad played football, he was the best
He was better than all the rest
At one point, someone cut open his knee
Him and his dad, weren't very happy.

He got a tackle on his kneecap, studs and all
Then my dad's professional dreams started to fall
Now my dad manages my team
Inspiring us all to go for our dream.

Adam Whiteley (13)
Baines School, Poulton-le-Fylde

Nelson Mandela

Times were bad in South Africa,
Blacks and whites were not equal,
Then Nelson Mandela came along,
To correct all the wrong.

The whites locked him in prison,
Twenty-five years in captivity,
The whites saw him as a threat,
He wouldn't be a threat in prison.

Concerts were held in his name,
To raise awareness, to ease the pain,
The whites let him out of prison,
A new age was born, no more division.

All because of this wonderful man,
Nobody is restricted, everybody can,
All his life he stood up for what he believed in,
The Apartheid now was gone, but AIDS and poverty live on.

Thomas Harding (12)
Baines School, Poulton-le-Fylde

Jacqueline Wilson

Jacqueline Wilson is my inspiration
Her books adorned throughout the nation
Her tales intrigue and entertain
And children read them again and again
Her writing so fluent with a touch of anticipation
Her next books awaited with much expectation.

When I am older, I dream to write
Books that humour and excite
Tales about love and devotion
Tales that trigger your emotion
And nobody does this better throughout the nation
Than Jacqueline Wilson, my inspiration!

Rebecca Ingham (13)
Baines School, Poulton-le-Fylde

I Have A Dream

It takes a lot to change mankind,
To turn the world around,
Black and white can live together,
Now equality has been found.

'I have a dream . . .' is what he said,
Four words which meant so much,
Now life is good for everyone,
A very special touch.

Before the world was divided up,
Into the different races,
Fights broke out and wars began,
In many different places.

What's the different between black and white?
The answer is nothing at all
And now we have all realised this,
We have answered this special man's call.

Now from Africa to England,
Mankind's life is slowly improving,
We have one person to thank for all this . . .
Martin Luther King.

Emily Cook (13)
Baines School, Poulton-le-Fylde

Grandma

G randma is my idol because she can do things other grannies can't
R uns around like a ten-year-old, especially when it's the start of
                                                  Coronation Street
A nd she makes me laugh silly when she's dancing
N othing can stop her from smiling all the time
D id you know she's a better cook than Gordon Ramsay and reads
                                                  hundreds of books a week
M P3 player is her latest thing, as well as her flash computer
A ll the things I can do, Granny can do better.

Tom Johnson (13)
Baines School, Poulton-le-Fylde

Nelson Mandela

Before him, there was discrimination,
Nothing but a silent nation,
A racial divide that was so great,
That the whole world was filled with hate.

He dreamed of equal rights,
Black and white to have peaceful nights,
How could colour cause so much misery?
It doesn't matter, why could they not see?

He fought so hard, all his life,
Twenty-five years with conditions so rife,
He couldn't be stopped, so they threw away the key,
But he kept on fighting until he was free.

He inspired the world to never give up,
To be individual isn't so tough,
He is my role model to speak my mind,
To keep on fighting and to put my troubles behind.

Georgina Gerrard (13)
Baines School, Poulton-le-Fylde

My Spectacular Single Parent

Don't you *ever* dare think single parents are scum,
Half my childhood's been led by my spectacular mum.

I have grown up watching her work till she drops,
Relentlessly, selflessly pulling out all the stops.

We might have caravan holidays and a battered old car,
But just one loving parent is enough to make you go far.

She doesn't claim benefits, smoke, booze or take any drugs,
Just drinks gallons of tea from one of her favourite mugs.

What an inspiration she has been to me and my brother,
The world is at my feet and it's all down to my mother.

Chad Booth (13)
Baines School, Poulton-le-Fylde

Faultless, Fabulous Not Famous

My role models aren't famous,
They're not known by the press,
But they're my inspirations,
They'll never be anything less.

They cheer me up when I am blue,
They make me laugh and smile
And all five of my idols,
Will always be worthwhile.

Each of them are different,
They all have diverse ways,
To make me feel so special,
When I'm in a daze.

So each of my role models,
Can help me round the bend,
Of life itself, my idols are,
My faultless, fabulous friends!

Hayley Blofeld (12)
Baines School, Poulton-le-Fylde

To Be Like David Beckham

You've inspired the world with your technique
And wowed all the girls with your cute physique
So many people look up to you
Your skills are just legend through and through
People wear a number seven shirt with pride
But you just take it all in your stride
You hit the target when taking a free kick
You're so good, it makes some people sick
The world would love to do what you do,
This poem was described and written for you.

Sharna Guest-Crossley (13)
Baines School, Poulton-le-Fylde

My Dream

To be a footballer is my dream,
To be like you and play for the England team,
To do lots of tricks and score goals too,
To be cheered on the pitch and cross balls like you.

I love the way you style your hair,
The way you play and use your flare,
You are my inspiration I look up to you,
Although you have your drawbacks and your moments too.

When you shoot, you never miss,
Your talent is top of the football list,
I love your fashion sense and the boots you've bought,
I think you're the king of your sport.

The skills you use are ever so slick,
You can spin round defenders and run ever so quick,
When you play for England, you are number seven,
The football god of free kicks that plays and lives in Heaven.

When I grow up I want to be just like you,
Be the best in the world and play like it too.

Shee Mwazanzale (12)
Baines School, Poulton-le-Fylde

I Have A Dream

My nan is one in a million,
She means everything to me
She's my role model
And makes me so happy
She's been through the worst
With cancer twice
Maybe it's a curse,
For just being nice
She's up in the sky,
Harmed no more,
I hope she realises
That I love her more than I did before.

Chantelle Preece (12)
Baines School, Poulton-le-Fylde

My Inspiration

My sister inspires me, she does,
She hasn't done anything spectacular,
Like many other people,
But my sister is always there for me.

My sister used to scare me,
In fact, she still does,
Although my sister scares me,
She is the best sister possible.

My sister is a great person,
Who inspires me to lead a good life,
As she leads a good life
And tries to do right by everyone.

My sister was bullied at school
And wasn't a high achiever,
But she struggled through,
To be the great person she is today.

I also have two other sisters and a brother,
Who inspire me as well,
But my sister, Catherine,
Is the one leading me down the right path.

Kerry Steen (13)
Baines School, Poulton-le-Fylde

Who's Your Inspiration?

Who inspires you? Who inspires me?
Is it Martin Luther King or Mahatma Gandhi?
Both men helped to change the world.

Is it someone more modern?
Someone who helps you learn?
Or is it someone who inspires you to go and change the world?

Is your role model a footballer or is your role model a singer?
Are they really an inspiration or are they just simply a winner?
Anyone can be a role model, all you've got to do is try.

It may be your parents who inspire you,
It could be one person or maybe even two,
Whoever it is, *you* decide.

So who really is your inspiration?
Does someone fill you with pride and elation
When you think of how they went and changed the world?

It doesn't matter if you're a boy or a girl,
You too can go and change the world,
You can do it if you have a dream.

Laura Scott (12)
Baines School, Poulton-le-Fylde

Who Inspires Me?

Who inspires me? Well, I'll tell you,
He's mega funny and is always there for me,
If I ever need money to go to the shops,
I'd ask him and he'd hand it over, then go back to his tea.

If me and my sister were fighting,
He'd break us up, but never shout,
Well, not at me anyway,
He'd stick up for me, without a doubt.

If I did bad at school,
He'd be disappointed of course
And he'd tell me to do better next time
And I'd work with better source.

But as you asked, 'Who inspires me?'
Well, as I said, I would tell,
But the person who inspires me,
Is my dad, the person at who I'd never yell.

Gemma Fallon (13)
Baines School, Poulton-le-Fylde

Roald Dahl

Ever since the age of three,
Roald Dahl has inspired me,
Exciting tales for young and old,
As each page turns, a plot unfolds,
A breath of magic in every word,
Each story needing to be heard,
Sitting in his mother's chair,
Scribbling ideas down without a care,
From little minpins who live in trees,
To men who own chocolate factories!
Delighting children every time,
The final project, full of rhyme,
Roald Dahl has inspired me,
Ever since the age of three.

Maisie Mitchell (13)
Baines School, Poulton-le-Fylde

My Inspiration

With a beep and a flash,
There's a leap and a splash,
The weight of the world on his shoulders.

Racing down the pool,
At a pace that's so cruel,
Going for gold like he told us.

Swimming backstroke, then fly,
He whizzes on by,
Like no other swimmer before him.

He's a phalange from gold,
We hope he won't fold,
With the pressure put on him by Klim.

Known worldwide for total domination,
Michael Phelps is my inspiration.

Jack Stanney (13)
Baines School, Poulton-le-Fylde

Bruce Lee

Bruce Lee is a very great man,
Try to fight him, I doubt that you can,
Flips and kicks through the air,
He makes you want to stop and stare,
He stars in movies, blockbusters and more,
Watch very carefully and you'll see what he has in store,
He shows off his knowledge of martial arts well,
Defeating another man is just another story he can tell,
He isn't very big, but he's definitely hard,
Battered and bruised and mentally scarred,
But still he fights on, during night and day,
He has a reputation for carrying on anyway,
When he was old, he was no weaker than before,
He would carry on until he could fight no more,
My inspiration is definitely Bruce Lee,
He's the man that I want to be.

Luke Sanderson (13)
Baines School, Poulton-le-Fylde

Thierry Henry

He's as smooth as a butterfly
And he glides like a bee
You'll never tackle him
Cos 'him' is Thierry Henry.

Foot to the ball
Curling to the net
Starts to dip in
The keeper has found a threat.

Crosses and shots
He creates the chances
The keeper can only watch
This golden player, as he dances.

Henry at the corner
A man with a soul
Chips one in the box
A nut in the goal.

Celebration!
Qualification!
Golden glory!
Relaxation!

For the team
For the country
For the cup . . .
Thierry Henry.

Richard Gupta (12)
Baines School, Poulton-le-Fylde

An Inspiration

Mohammed Ali is an inspiration,
He inspires me,
He fights like a butterfly,
Stings like a bee.

He stands up for many people,
No matter who they be,
Black or white, rich or poor,
There's no differences to see.

He may be young,
But be does not care,
He can seduce his opponent,
In one single stare.

He's shown that you can have the power,
To be who you want to be,
To stand for what you believe in
And set the crowd's spirits free.

Mohammed Ali is an inspiration.

Georgia Noble (13)
Baines School, Poulton-le-Fylde

Inspiration Poem

This person showed us something,
That even with a deadly disease,
You can still live a normal life
And raise money for that disease.

He has cycled many marathons
And has raised hundreds,
Curing hundreds of people,
All around the country.

His name is Lance Armstrong,
Suffered from cancer whilst cycling
And still made it to the end
And he is my role model.

Nick Rosindale (13)
Baines School, Poulton-le-Fylde

I Have A Dream

The person who inspires me is someone with little fame,
Katherine Sidebottom is her name,
She lived for 93 years, helping and giving
And didn't mind how much she got for a living
As long as she helped and cared,
She wasn't bothered how well she fared
She worked in a charity called Meals on Wheels
And for free, cooked poor people meals
For all her kindness she got a medal from the Queen,
It was hard for people to believe who she'd seen
Her prize MBE stood for Member of the British Empire,
Believe me on this, I am no liar
This person is my mum's godmother,
She was so kind that everyone loved her
But then she got so old and helpless,
Even then she didn't help people less,
Now she's dead, my mum's godmother,
But in my heart, I will always remember her.

Cameron Woodall (13)
Baines School, Poulton-le-Fylde

Bob Geldof

Poverty was increasing, many on the streets,
Diseases and illness took over in fleets,
The poor people of Africa, no money, no food,
But as this one man came, conditions improved.

Spirits lifting, moral rising,
This one man was very enterprising,
He came with some money,
He came with a cheque, the gift of life no one could ever forget.

A musician by trade,
His friends he did persuade,
To join him in forming the band for Live Aid,
Raising lots of money for the people he hoped to save.

Twenty years passed,
His mission incomplete,
So they introduced Live 8, as a repeat.

Their goal was no mystery,
All they wanted to do, was make poverty history!

Lauren Stott (13)
Baines School, Poulton-le-Fylde

A Poem About Pelé

He took the Brazilians to a World Cup win,
He wasn't the biggest player, in fact very slim,
His talent and pace was outstanding,
He didn't need to be commanding.

When he quit the game, millions were sad,
He made great defenders looks so bad,
With a turn and a flick,
He was gone in a tick.

He was breathtaking, with a ball at his feet,
He just made everything look so neat,
Let's just say he's a living great,
He still will be, at a later date.

Let's just face it, he was amazing,
In rain or when the sun was blazing,
I have only been lucky enough to see him on the telly,
His name . . . the incredible *Pelé!*

Matthew Hunt (13)
Baines School, Poulton-le-Fylde

The Unknown Soldier

Valiant, brave, courageous and bold,
The one whose tale cannot be told,
The one whose life was lost in war,
The one who's lost for evermore.

Through selflessness he gave his life,
Battling on through pain and strife,
Fear and horror knew no bounds,
In no-man's-land of muddy ground.

The enemy he faced that day,
Would not have known him anyway,
Shells and bullets flew thick and fast,
Death was swift, a mighty blast.

That tore his body so much, it's true,
For his family, a grave, they never knew,
Truly no greater inspiration there be,
A person so young, to die for me.

Rosie Keighley (13)
Baines School, Poulton-le-Fylde

Inspiration

He inspires many young children across the whole of the world,
Amazing his opponents with new tricks and flicks,
He is the entertainer of the football world.

He controls the ground he plays on, while the whole world glares,
He inspires me to play, because of the magic he shares,
The moment I see him with the ball at his feet,
I can't stop myself from playing in rain or heat.

The Brazilian magician has the feet of God,
He plays beautiful football in the yellow Brazil
And beautiful football in the Camp Nou of the mighty Barcelona.

Ronaldinho the great is the true inspiration of the beautiful game,
Thousands of children are hypnotised to try to be the same,
Maybe one day in my dreams, I could step onto the field with the legend,
Or to clean his boots would be a pleasure.

He was raised in Porto Alegre as Ronaldo de Assis Moreira,
But we know him as Mr Ronaldinho,
He plays with a smile and he has a spirit like no other.

A role model of the best
And to me, better than all the rest,
Never give up, try your best, be unique and entertain,
This typifies my role model and the man I look up to.

There is no other like him, no other who can amaze the world,
No other who makes football look so easy
And no other who I dream about playing like.
Joga Bonito my friends.

Ronaldinho!

Liam Roache (13)
Baines School, Poulton-le-Fylde

I Have A Dream . . . One Day

I have a dream . . .
That one day everyone lives the same life.

I have a dream . . .
That one day the world will be at peace.

I have a dream . . .
That one day everyone has equal rights.

I have a dream . . .
That one day we all live in happiness.

I have a dream . . .
That one day I will find happiness.

I have a dream . . .
That one day I will make people proud.

I have a dream . . .
That one day my dream comes true!

Leanne Postlethwaite (14)
Cansfield High School, Wigan

I Have A Dream

I often dream of a world of equality
With no titles like 'chav' or 'sweedy'

A world with no name-calling
Where problems are solved by talking

I know this world could never exist
If it did it would be lost in the mist

You cannot blame someone for dreaming
Of a world where every face is beaming.

Lewis Henderson (13)
Cansfield High School, Wigan

My One And Only Wish

The way they stare,
Paranoia strikes me,
Do they really care?
Is this what they want to see?

Druid, disturbing, drizzling days pass by,
They stole the light, wrapped it up tight,
On the inside I die,
One day I might not have to see this sight.

Can you bring me down anymore?
This isn't what I wanted,
It's not what I planned for,
I'm not the only one, but their ways are firmly planted.

Just to be me,
To not worry about anything else,
I only wish they could see,
How much they come across false.

Wishing on it never makes it comes true,
But what am I supposed to do?
They're ready to *attack* again, travelling in their herds,
I'll be OK as long as I remember . . .
Actions speak louder than words!

Rose Williams (13)
Cansfield High School, Wigan

One Person, One Voice

One person who is the light in the darkness
One person who has the courage of a lion
One person who has a voice loud enough to spread the word
One voice that can be the peace in the war-stricken world
One voice that can right the wrongs
One voice that has the volume to speak up
In a crowd full of nobodies and everybodies
One person, one voice to say, 'I have a dream'
Can change the world!

Robyn Sharpe (14)
Cansfield High School, Wigan

I Have A Dream

When you walk down the street
Have you ever seen
The way that people look at you
For the clothes you wear?

Have you ever noticed
And have you ever thought
What it would be like
To be accepted?

Have you ever dreamed
Of being noticed for you
And have you ever dreamed
Of walking freely?

Have you ever dreamed
That you can walk free
Without being threatened
And without facing death?

This is a dream
A dream that is simple
To be accepted
For who you really are . . .

Allanah Riley (14)
Cansfield High School, Wigan

I Have A Dream!

How many times have you seen a person walking down the street?
How many times have you judged them for the colour of their skin?
How many times have you judged them for the way they look?
How many times have you seen other people do the same thing?
How many times have you wanted to say something?
How many times have actually said something?
Never!
Now is your chance to say something
Now is your chance to tell them to get on with their lives.

Charlotte Richards (13)
Cansfield High School, Wigan

I Have A Dream To Be An Athlete

I have a dream . . .
That one day I could win the gold
I have a dream . . .
That I could be a dame, be loved, be supported
I have a dream . . .
I could run the track for my country
I have a dream . . .
That I could live to be loved
I have a dream . . .
That I could be cheered all the way to happiness
I have a dream . . .
That I could pass the finish in a winning time
I have a dream . . .
That I can make my country proud
I have a dream . . .
To run like Kelly Holmes
I have a dream . . .
To make my family proud
To always please the crowd
To win the Olympic gold
To always be told

I have a dream . . .
That everyone could fulfil their goals.

Aimee Dalton (14)
Cansfield High School, Wigan

I Have A Dream

Testing on animals is cruel,
Needles are injected
And no creatures are rejected,
It causes lots of pain,
Are people going insane?

This is what I dream,
Get rid of this wicked scene.

Ears have been grown
And all of this is known,
Yet testing still goes on,
Whilst animals' happiness has gone.

Lipstick, creams and blusher
Are just a few of which I'll cover
They cause nasty rashes and others
Of which are horrible to suffer.

All of this for variety
When animals lose their sanity
Help put a stop to this now
But I'd better tell you how.

Look at adverts in some books
Or browse online and have a look
This is what I dream
Get rid of this wicked scene.

Jodie Wadsworth (14)
Cansfield High School, Wigan

The Bully And His Follower

The world is full of people
Set out to bring us down
They tease, torment and torture us
And replace our smile with a frown.

You'd think they'd have something better to do
Than make our lives hell
They punch us down to the ground
Then tell everyone we fell.

But one day they'll meet their match
Someone twice as big
They'll bring us all to glory
By slaughtering the pig.

Until that day, we'll have to
Take it like a man
The bully and his follower
Following him like a lamb.

Ryan Dickinson (14)
Cansfield High School, Wigan

My Dream . . .

I have a dream . . .
That one day we will all live in harmony
I have a dream . . .
That one day people of the world won't judge
I have a dream . . .
That maybe someday we will live in peace
I have a dream . . .
That one day all goals will be achieved
I have a dream . . .
That one day wishes become reality
I have a dream . . .
That maybe someday we will live in peace
I have a dream . . .
That one day a voice will be heard
I have a dream . . .
That one day violence will not be known
I have a dream . . .
That maybe someday we will live in peace!

Yasmin Houghton (14)
Cansfield High School, Wigan

I Have A Dream

I have a dream . . .
That people will be truthful and trustworthy
I have a dream . . .
That everyone will have equal rights and live happily
I have a dream . . .
That injustice ends
I have a dream . . .
That everyone gets a fair chance in life
I have a dream . . .
That every race is accepted
I have a dream . . .
That peace ends all arguments
I have a dream . . .
That people will not kill or hurt creatures for vanity
I have a dream . . .
That families grow old together in peace
I have a dream . . .
That love is no longer false and finally becomes real!

Ayesha Abouharous (14)
Cansfield High School, Wigan

Stop Bullying

S is for sadness which I feel
T is for tears trickling down my face
O is for offending which they do to me
P is for picking on me

B is for bullying and how horrible it is
U is for upset which is what I always feel like
L is for lying which they do when confronted
L is for laughing when they see I am upset
Y is for, 'Why me?'
I is for ignoring me which I would rather they would do
N is for nasty which is the names they call me
G is for ganging up on people.

Stop bullying!

Liam Tomkinson (13)
Coppenhall High School, Crewe

My Friends

I will always have friends, how do I know?
I always know, I know I have,
My friends never ever betray me,
They never leave me alone, on my own.

They are my real friends, they're not humans;
Human friends always talk behind my back,
They're always two-faced,
Even though they don't act it.

My real friends speak,
They aren't like a bird just moving its beak,
I can understand their language,
Even though no one else does.

I always have this dream;
The dream I've talked above,
Those friends are beside me all the time,
They're always, always silent,
Their silence means everything.

Friends!

Ella Su (12)
Coppenhall High School, Crewe

Racism

In this world, God created black and white
Why will they pick on them just because they're different colour?

Everyone is the same, colour does not matter
Kids don't deserve to get picked on

Why can't it just stop this minute
And the rest of the children can have a happy life?

Don't ruin your own life!

Dean Burrows (11)
Coppenhall High School, Crewe

I Have A Dream

I have a dream that the world was safe,
We'd be proud to be the human race,
If no one steals and no one lies,
There would be no need for cops or spies.

Where all the blacks and all the whites,
Could be friends and could unite,
A world where no one really cares,
About your looks or clothes you wear.

Where every person on the street,
Gets a job and gets back on their feet,
Where there's no tears and no regrets,
Where no one cries and no one frets.

No one has to be upset,
The world is not over yet,
So there's still time for us to prove,
That we can stop being rude,
That we can stop being mean
And everyone can join a team.

If every person in the world,
Respected every boy and girl,
Each teacher, mum and brother too,
Maybe then they would respect you.

Danyel Faddes (13)
Coppenhall High School, Crewe

I Have A Dream

I have a dream . . .
When I'm older I will play for Liverpool
I have a dream . . .
I will become the Golden Boot winner in the Premiership
I have a dream . . .
I will play alongside Steven Gerrard
I have a dream

I have a dream . . .
I will be the fans' favourite
I will wear the shirt with pride
I have a dream . . .
That I will be the top goal scorer ever for Liverpool
And score the winning goal in the FA Cup final
I have a dream . . .
That the fans will chant my name all around Anfield
I have a dream . . .
I will become the Liverpool captain
I have a dream

I have a dream . . .
I will play in the Champions League final
And beat Manchester United
I have a dream . . .
I will beat Man Utd, Chelsea and Arsenal, 3-0
I will lift the Premiership Cup
I have a dream.

Daniel Holland (13)
Coppenhall High School, Crewe

I Have A Dream

I have a dream . . .
Of no one fighting
Instead they should be hiking
No husbands and wives shouting
Or one of them will leave.

I have a dream . . .
Where there were no wars
Because fighting might kill someone
And then they will be gone for good.

I have a dream . . .
Of black and white people working together
So then there will be no racism forever.

I have a dream . . .
That the world isn't polluted
Just a clean world
So we can take care of the world
Together, *forever!*

Daniel Corbett (13)
Coppenhall High School, Crewe

A Dream

A dream for me would be
To save our world of dying children, you see
From starvation
To devastation from neglect to abuse

Yes, when I become a big person
I will do my best to make things right
So many little children can see the light

I would like to take away their pain
So they can play and have fun again
They don't need lots of money or presents too
They just need lots of love from me and you.

Lauren Wheatley (11)
Coppenhall High School, Crewe

Racism

In this world, God made us humans
To respect each other for who we are
And *not* for the colour of our skin.

Everyone is different
But we should all be treated the same
And *not* for the colour of our skin.

Black people are just the same
As white people
It is the skin that is different.

Just stop and think how you would react
If you were treated the same as black people
Having to get on different buses, the not so good ones
And think if every white person crossed the road
To get away from you.

Scott Bebbington (12)
Coppenhall High School, Crewe

Things That Matter

You always keep good memories from your past,
When you think about life, it goes quite fast,
Days go by, nights come and go,
When things go bad, it goes very slow.

Things that matter to me will always stay
They will come back and thank me one day,
Like family and friends and people who care,
The world should share kindness, that's in the air.

War is sick and should never be allowed,
Every country should stand and be proud,
Nature and animals should never be abused,
Fur and skin should never be misused.

So let things that matter
Be number one.

Amy Heath (13)
Coppenhall High School, Crewe

Bullying Is Bad

In the playground,
Or on the street,
No one likes a bully.
Bullies are like a bullet to the heart,
Hurt you when you are down.
Would you like to be bullied?
I didn't think so!
Stop it right now!

Sian Lewis (12)
Coppenhall High School, Crewe

Bullying

B ullying should stop
U nderstand each other
L ove each other
L isten to each other
Y es, that's right
I gnore each other
N o, that's wrong
G o together, stick together.

Emily Piotrowicz (12)
Coppenhall High School, Crewe

Just Imagine

Imagine a . . .
Peaceful and warless world
Imagine a . . .
World free for every race and religion
Instead of . . .
Seeing the poor children in Africa
Starve on a few grains of rice
This is all they eat every day
This should not be the way.

Jordan Foster (13)
Coppenhall High School, Crewe

The World Cup

I have a dream . . .
That England will win the World Cup
But it is very doubtful.

I have a dream . . .
That Brazil will lose to England
In the final.

I have a dream . . .
That Joe Cole
Will get the Golden Boot for England.

I have a dream . . .
That Brazil
Will come runners-up to England.

I have a dream . . .
That Michael Owen
Will be back in full training for the rest of the World Cup.

I have a dream . . .
That Michael Owen
Will be playing amazingly
In the World Cup final.

Zaheer Ahmed (13)
Coppenhall High School, Crewe

Bully

Don't bully in the playground
Don't bully in the street
Don't bully anywhere

No one likes a bully
Don't bully anywhere

If you're a bully, stop it now
Don't bully anywhere!

Chelsea Louise Latham (12)
Coppenhall High School, Crewe

Sporting Legend

I have a dream . . .
I have scored
The winning goal
In the World Cup final.

I have a dream . . .
I have served
The winning ace
In the Wimbledon final.

I have a dream . . .
I have scored a drop-kick
To win the
Rugby Six Nations.

I have a dream . . .
I have scored
A slam-dunk
To win the NBA.

I have dream . . .
I have beaten
The world record for the 100m
In the Olympic final.

I have a dream . . .
I have taken
The last wicket
To win the Ashes.

I have a dream . . .
In my dream
I am a
Sporting legend!

Dale Bradbury (13)
Coppenhall High School, Crewe

I Have A Dream

I have a dream . . .
Everyone would get along
And everyone's friendship would be strong

I have a dream . . .
White met black
And all the fights won't strike back

I have a dream . . .
Everyone would not fight
And all the love stayed at night

I have a dream . . .
There wouldn't be war, stress and strife
Why would someone want to lose their life?

I have a dream . . .
Everyone would get along
And everyone's friendship would be strong!

Leanne-Marie Clulow (13)
Coppenhall High School, Crewe

Family

F amilies are great
A ll the time
M ums give birth to you
 I n great joy, waiting to love you
L ying in bed at night all of your family dream about you
Y ou are important to everyone

Dads are the ones
That help look after you
Day and night
And make sure you don't get hurt
You are special to your family
So you should make them
Feel special too.

Alice Holme (12)
Coppenhall High School, Crewe

War

Why does war start?
It tears people apart
There is no need for war
It's just a big bore.

As parents die
Their children just hold and cry
War is an argument gone wrong
Why can't people just get along?
Why can't people just live in peace
Instead of conflict?
I say to you now, stop all this hate
Otherwise, violence will escalate.

Dominick Kershaw (13)
Coppenhall High School, Crewe

Imagine

Imagine . . .
A world free of poaching,
Imagine . . .
A world free of animal cruelty,
A world free of these horrible and terrible deeds
Would be a much better place to live,
Imagine . . .
A world free of whaling
If it were free to stop
It would be plain sailing
Would be a much better place,
Imagine . . .
People protesting about animal testing
It never works
But together we can stop this *now!*

Jessica Robinson (13)
Coppenhall High School, Crewe

Animal Cruelty

Whimpering and crying
Slowly dying
Pets of all ages
Imprisoned in cages

Injections and jabs
Medication and tabs
Suffering with pain
The whole thing's insane

Make-up and perfume
Just to look nice
These things have been tested
On cute little mice

In the twenty-first century
This should not be
Because I would not like it
If that were me!

Charlene Quail (14)
Coppenhall High School, Crewe

Stop

Here's a warning
About global warming
It is ruining our land
Our beautiful land
I care
Let's make a pair
In one hundred years
We will all be in tears
When our land
Our beautiful land
Will no longer be here.

Peter Clews (12)
Coppenhall High School, Crewe

My Name Is Sarah

I am here today to talk to you about child abuse and murder
This is how it starts, *I want it to stop*
My name is Sarah and I am three,
My eyes are swollen, I cannot see,
I must be stupid, I must be bad,
What else could have made my daddy so mad?
I wish I were better, I wish I wasn't ugly,
Then maybe my mummy would still hug me,
When I'm awake I'm all alone,
The house it's dark, my folks aren't home,
When my mummy does come, I'll try to be nice,
So maybe I'll just get one whipping tonight,
I just heard a car, my daddy is home,
I hear him curse my name, he bawls,
I press myself against the hard wall,
I try and hide myself from his evil eyes,
I'm afraid now, I start to cry,
He finds me weeping and shouts nasty words,
He says it's my fault he suffers at work,
He slaps me and hits me and yells at me more,
I finally get free and run for the door,
He's already locked it and I start to bawl,
He gets me and throws me against the hard wall
And he stops and heads for the door,
While I lay there, sprawled on the floor,
I wish my daddy would stop abusing me,
My name is Sarah and I am three
And tonight my daddy murdered me.

Jodie Pogonowski (12)
Coppenhall High School, Crewe

I Have A Dream

It was a good game
Apparently
Liverpool won
Apparently
We won on penalties
Apparently
I didn't watch Liverpool win
Definitely
I saw people shouting offensively
Definitely
I saw racism and discrimination
Definitely
I saw the police arresting
Definitely
I smelt and heard excess amounts of alcohol
I saw Liverpool lose
Definitely
I heard the people playing for Liverpool won
Will it ever be possible that
We can celebrate as a race rather than a team?
Will it ever be possible that
We can have a good time without the police?
Will it be possible that
We can unite in friendship with our opponents?
The sad thing is it is very possible and not hard!

Kristoffer Geyer (13)
Gateacre Community Comprehensive School, Liverpool

I Have A Dream . . .

I have a dream . . .
That one day opposites will be equal
That people, no matter how tall, small, fat or thin
Will unite to help all the people of the world

I have a dream . . .
That poverty and crime will stop
Wars and battles will never start
So families will not drift apart

I have a dream . . .
That racism will never happen
Murder, genocide and killing will end
So that there will be peace throughout

I have a dream . . .
That one day crime and evil will never happen
And Mother Nature will help us survive
The nightmares of our world

I have a dream . . .
That we can all live together in peace
And
That one day that dream will become reality.

Tom Simpson (13)
Gateacre Community Comprehensive School, Liverpool

Feeling Lonely

Never feeling lonely is a hard thing to do,
Except for those lucky few,
With money and happiness all year round,
Yet there are people who have no money or happiness
Thinking they are on their own.

You are born with an intention to be sad or lonely
Once in a lifetime,
But remember,
There is always someone there to help.

Martin Hazzard (13)
Gateacre Community Comprehensive School, Liverpool

I Have A Dream . . .

I have a dream . . .
That bullying will stop
People following the crowd
They shouldn't be so proud
Because these kids have no silver lining
To the cloud.

Don't kick them down, pick them up
Are they so different
They have to suffer?
Leave them alone
They haven't done anything wrong
Don't make their lives any tougher.

Never forget that you and them are the same
So why bully, skit and hate?
You could even find yourself a new mate
So even if your friends think it's cool
Think about it, it's just cruel . . .

Dean Norbury (14)
Gateacre Community Comprehensive School, Liverpool

I Have A Dream . . .

I have a dream . . .
That the Earth would stop
Punishing innocent people.

The hurricane Katrina
Demolished people's lives,
Not only their homes.

And they can look
For no one to blame,
Not even themselves.

Lauren Donnelly (14)
Gateacre Community Comprehensive School, Liverpool

I Have A Dream

No violence
No danger
No racism
Let's call it quits with terrorism

No bombs
No guns
No knifes
Let's just get on and live our lives

No drugs
No weed
No drink
Let's all try and keep our livers pink

No name-calling
No punching
No stealing
Let's all keep on believing!

Ellis Williams (14)
Gateacre Community Comprehensive School, Liverpool

I Have A Dream . . .

Caring and sharing is what the world's about,
No shouting, no stabbing, nobody getting knocked out,
Being nice is the main thing and that's what we should do,
Because if you're nasty, someone could be the same to you.

Hurting and swearing should be the last thing on your mind,
The world would be a better place without
I think you would find.

Hannah Finnigan (14)
Gateacre Community Comprehensive School, Liverpool

I Have A Dream

Bullies look around you
I don't know them
But they know me
If you don't say anything
They will get you more
Adults say,
'They do it to look big.'
I think they're cowards
I try to act myself
By answering back
I get scared and walk away
I just keep it to myself
And get bullied more
So one day
I hope it all ends.

Nataleigh Williamson (14)
Gateacre Community Comprehensive School, Liverpool

My Dream

My dream is that all the people in the world
Can live in peace,
All the people in the world don't fight,
All the people in the world are right,
Everyone in the world shouldn't lie,
Everyone in the would shouldn't cry,
The whole world shouldn't be sad,
The whole world shouldn't be bad,
God's world should be looked after,
God's world should have lots of laughter.

Louis Maddison (14)
Gateacre Community Comprehensive School, Liverpool

I Have A Dream . . .

I have a dream . . .
That everyone can feel equal
And no one will be left out
No racism in the world
No singling people out
I believe that everyone should have the right
To express his or her feelings about something
Able to wear the clothes they like
Whether it is because of their religion
Or if they just like it
I have a dream . . .
That everyone should have the right
To believe in their own religion
Without anyone making any bad comments about it
People should just be able to live their lives
How they want
Not what other people want them to do
I have a dream . . .
That there should be peace in the world
Such as no wars and no religious comments
I have a dream . . .
That all this becomes reality.

Conner Jones (13)
Gateacre Community Comprehensive School, Liverpool

I Have A Dream . . .

I have a dream . . .
That the world was so perfect
And there would just be peace

I have a dream . . .
That no one was homeless,
Left out or unloved

I have a dream . . .
That no child is bullied
Or abused in any way

I have a dream . . .
That there is no more poverty
And that I could lock a door
And everyone would be safe

I have a dream . . .
That we are all friends
And that wars could not go on

I have a dream . . .
That no one is poor
And no racism goes on

Well, I had that dream
Just one day, could that come true?
Will any of it come true?

Zoe Lawson (13)
Gateacre Community Comprehensive School, Liverpool

I Have A Dream . . .

I have a dream . . .
The world is more safe
When I go out at night
I have a dream . . .
When you're alone
There is no more fright
I have a dream . . .
That when it gets dark
There is no old man looking drunk in a park
I have a dream . . .
That when you're in school
There are no bullies that make you look like a fool
I have a dream . . .
That I don't have to pray when it comes to the end
Of the day
I have a dream.

Laura Spruce (14)
Gateacre Community Comprehensive School, Liverpool

I Had A Dream

I had a dream where people don't need money
Back in my days there were no civil wars
Now bullies are just weak
But it takes courage to stand up to one
If there's no war
There's no need for weapons
Wouldn't it be nice if there was no racism and bullying?
It would be class if everyone had some kind of transport
Wouldn't it be nice if there were smiles
All around the world?
Wouldn't it be nice if there were no drugs in the world?
It would be nice if the houses and taxes were free
I want no more gang wars or drugs
I want everyone to have clean water supplies
And food all over the world.

Jonathan Barton (12)
Lostock Hall Community High School, Preston

I Have A Dream

I f only the world had no war

H appiness would be all around
A lthough the world is full of bullies
V enture into another place
E verywhere is in disgrace

A nger, murder, vengeances and threat

D isobeying isn't right
R acism should be no more
E veryone should get along
A nyone can fulfil their dreams
M oney should be used in the right way

F amilies should respect each other
O lder people should be cared for
R emember the people who have come and gone

T owns and cities should not be dull
H ungry people should be fed
E verybody should be kind

W ar is vile and cruel
O ver the years that are going by
R ed blood should never be seen
L ove should be all around
D reams should be true

T errorists should stop
O thers should think for themselves

B ored children should have something to do
E ducation for me and you

B abies should all be fed
E veryone should get what they want
T rees should get the same choice
T ry to see eye to eye
E veryone deserves equal opportunities
R eligion should not be a barrier.

Jayne Threlfall (12)
Lostock Hall Community High School, Preston

I Have A Dream

I have a dream of freedom
For everyone alive
And I have a dream to give help
To those in desperate need
I have a dream

No matter the colour of the skin
Or what they may look like
It is in the heart that counts
And always will be
I have a dream

I have a dream of freedom
For everyone alive
And I have a dream to give help
To those in desperate need
I have a dream

No one should feel scared
Wherever they are
And everyone should have their friends
Either in body or in mind
I have a dream

I have a dream of freedom
For everyone alive
And I have a dream to give help
To those is desperate need
I have a dream

So let's unite together
And make these dreams come true
And make the world a better place
And give people a new start in life
I have a dream.

Samuel Caunce (13)
Lostock Hall Community High School, Preston

I Have A Dream . . .

I have a dream . . .
That my friends and family
Will not get bullied
And that one day
They will stand up to bullies.

I have a dream . . .
That people were fair
And kind in the world.

I have a dream . . .
That poor people could be rich
And that they have food to eat
And water to drink.

I have a dream . . .
That there was no violence
Or crime or bad people
In the world.

I have a dream . . .
That all the bad people in the world
Get put in a rocket
And shot off into space!

I have a dream . . .
That people try, try, try
And never give up.

I have a dream . . .
That everyone was safe
And not frightened.

All my dreams, I wish would come true
I wish everyone had my dreams too.

Rachel Smith (12)
Lostock Hall Community High School, Preston

I Have A Dream . . .

I have a dream . . .
Of world peace
We need to think for ourselves
Don't let others think for you.

I have a dream . . .
That people are treated fairly
We need to stand up for ourselves
Don't sit and hide in a corner.

I have a dream . . .
That there will be no more bullying
We need to try and get along
Don't hurt others.

I have a dream . . .
Of no more fights
We need to be more considerate
Don't be violent.

I have a dream . . .
That there are no more police
We need to stop getting into trouble
Don't be the one that goes to prison.

I have a dream . . .
Of other countries together
We have to think of others
Don't be the one to start a war.

I have a dream . . .
Of kindness
We need to be kind
Don't be nasty.

I have a dream . . .
Of a nice environment
We need to care for the Earth
Don't jeopardise the situation.

I have a dream . . .
Of women prime ministers
We need to be fair
Don't be sexist.

I have a dream . . .
Of law changes
We need to think of the law
Don't be the odd one out.

Alice Corrigan (11)
Lostock Hall Community High School, Preston

I Have A Dream . . .

I have a dream . . .
That all war in the world will stop
And that all weapons are destroyed.

I have a dream . . .
That all people living on the streets
Will be given some food
And a place to stay.

I have a dream . . .
That no one will be in pain
And that no one has to go through bad times alone.

I have a dream . . .
That poorer countries with poor people
Get good educations
So they can do something in their lives.

I have a dream . . .
That no one is scared or frightened
Of things like walking past gangs of people at night.

I have a dream . . .
That other people in poor countries
Get treated the same as everyone else with *no* racism
And that they get paid fair prices for their crops.

Matthew Carr (12)
Lostock Hall Community High School, Preston

I Have A Dream . . .

I have a dream . . .
That animals would stop being killed for sport.
I have a dream . . .
That we will all wake up one morning
And all of the falling out, all of the wars would stop
And everybody would be friends.
I have a dream . . .
That the doctors and nurses can make a cure for all illnesses.
I have a dream . . .
That not one person was poor
And no one was rich and we all had the same amount of money
And everyone had a home.
I have a dream . . .
That mums and dads would not fight with each other
And never split up.
I have a dream . . .
That litter would go in bins
And not on the floor.
I have a dream . . .
That cruelty to animals would stop.
I have a dream . . .
That everybody would have food and drink
And no one would starve or be thirsty.
I have a dream . . .
That sweets and chocolates were good for you
So your teeth will not rot.
I have a dream . . .
That people will do a job and get paid for it
And not go home without being paid.

Samantha Curry (11)
Lostock Hall Community High School, Preston

I Have A Dream . . .

I have a dream . . .
That I could fly,
Way up into the sky,
Flapping my arms and kicking my legs,
Making sure I don't get flies stuck in my pegs.

I have a dream . . .
That I could jump high,
Remember not to break the pole by eating a chicken pie,
I would love to land in the colossal sponge mat,
But watching out for the sight of cats.

I have a dream . . .
That I could shop,
Right through the day until I drop,
I hate it when you take stuff back,
To hang again upon the rack.

I have a dream . . .
That there was peace in the world,
People wouldn't laugh at you if you had your hair curled,
Get rid of all the Third World places,
Build playgrounds so the children can have races.

I have a dream . . .
I could be on stage,
Show all my talents and scream with rage,
Singing and dancing,
Acting and prancing.

I have a dream.

Rebecca Gidley (12)
Lostock Hall Community High School, Preston

I Have A Dream

I have a dream that people will be accepted
And racism comes to an end
They won't judge a book by its cover.
That I will never be on my own
People always here beside me to catch my fall
I will always have people to rely on.
Never give up trying, you will get there in the end
Stop all violence
Bring peace and hope to the world
Abusing, murdering and raping is wrong
Follow your own mind, you will achieve
You are the pilot of your own life
Never try to be someone you're not
Just be yourself
People will accept you for who you are
Not who you want to be
Think of others, not just yourself
There are people out there who have nothing at all.

Natasha Thorpe (12)
Lostock Hall Community High School, Preston

I Have A Dream

I have a dream for children to be safe
And have enough food to survive,
To stand up and be brave to bullies,
Not to be frightened,
To try and succeed no matter what,
To have fun, yet get a good education,
To have clothes to last the winter,
To have a family to support you,
To make most of life while you have it,
To get out in the sunshine and relax,
To make peace with other countries,
To have people smiling, laughing, happy,
For the world to be non-violent and more friendly.

Robyn Davidson (12)
Lostock Hall Community High School, Preston

Pursue Your Dreams

Ever feel like you don't belong
With a sea of people around you
And you think that everyone's against you?
You think that talking to that person you trust will help,
But everyone takes it the wrong way
And thinks that there's something going on between you,
You're only friends,
You try to ignore people saying things to you day in, day out,
Until one day, it gets too much,
I have a dream, that there would be no bullies in the world,
Or no one cared what other people thought about them.

Love of your life gone,
Never to be seen again,
Pain, misery, pain is the way forward,
You can get over him, it will take time,
Will is the key,
If you see him, should you talk?
Tell them how you feel or let him go, you're afraid,
Letting him go is a lengthy process,
Talk to him, you and him might be together,
What should you do?
Friends, family all wondering what's wrong,
You won't tell as it's heartache for you,
In class all you can think about is him,
There must be a way not to think about him,
But your heart's broken from when that person
And your friends left you, it'll take time,
Hearts do heal,
I have a dream, that there would be more people having
                                        happily ever afters.

Around the world are people that are dying,
Dying due to weather, we need to change the way we live,
Don't pollute the world, use other ways of transport,
Recycle, do anything to save lives
As people are dying as wells, rivers, reservoirs are all dried up,
I have a dream, that there is no pain and misery in the world.

Katrina Embleton (14)
Lostock Hall Community High School, Preston

I Have A Dream

I have a dream . . .
That soon one day
The world will be a better place
Where children can grow up with happiness
And they can live in peace.
I have a dream . . .
That soon one day
Violence and crime would go away
That people would have no fear of fighting and shootings.
I have a dream . . .
That soon one day
There would be no bullying, people getting hurt
They could have the courage to stand up to their enemies.
I have a dream . . .
That soon one day
People will not get hurt or give up
That people were not so poor.
I have a dream . . .
That soon one day
People would all be even
There wouldn't be so many changes.
I have a dream . . .
That soon one day
The world would be fair
And a happy place
That so many people wouldn't live in fear.
I have a dream . . .
That soon one day
Everyone would get a chance to say what they think is right.
I have a dream . . .
That soon one day
Somebody would change things
And make things right.
I have a dream . . .
That soon one day
Racism is no more
That everyone gets along with each other.

I have a dream . . .
That soon one day
Everybody would care
To make the world a better place.

Hannah Russell (12)
Lostock Hall Community High School, Preston

I Have A Dream . . .

I have a dream . . .
That there will be no wars or nuclear bombs
I have a dream . . .
That there will be no racism in this world
Because of a person's creed or colour
I have a dream . . .
That there will be no bullies anymore
I have a dream . . .
That there will be no more murders in the world
I have a dream . . .
That people should just be allowed to stand up
For what they believe in
And have their rights
I have a dream . . .
That there will be no more deaths
Due to tornadoes, earthquakes, meteor blasts or tsunamis
I have a dream . . .
That children are educated when they are born
So they can get a good job
And they don't have to go to school
I have a dream . . .
That money was grown on trees
I have a dream . . .
That people could wish for things
And then it would just appear in front of them.

Harry Ryding (12)
Lostock Hall Community High School, Preston

Lonely Angel

Sit on a forgotten cloud,
Rainfall, from windows of the soul,
A re-occurring twinge where the heart lays limp.
Melodies never sounded so sweet.

Gentle drops lay on lap,
Feet dangle into never,
Repressed wings wish to spread,
Melodies never sounded so sweet.

Though surrounded he knows,
Boundaries lay thick,
Emotions; unable to connect,
Melodies never sounded so sweet.

He felt alone,
But then a golden glance aside,
He knew his song could help his world,
Melodies sound sweeter when you know who's singing.

Aimeé-Jai Dunlop (13)
Lostock Hall Community High School, Preston

I Have A Dream . . .

I have a dream . . .
That we will be able to swim
Into the core of the sun
And glide along the surface of Jupiter
Where the gravity is crushingly immense.
I could light a candle on Pluto
Where, as the candle would normally freeze in the atmosphere.
I could surf Saturn and its mighty rings.
I could ride the pressure of a black hole sucking everything in it
I have a dream . . .
I believe because dreams are the future.

Jake Warburton (12)
Lostock Hall Community High School, Preston

How Can We Change The World?

How can we change the world?
War and poverty are two of the greatest factors in this world
Is it the lack of understanding that is causing this
And has an impact on everyone and everything
But the answer is simple.

Communication.

Communication is the key factor in all aspects of life
If everyone from minorities learn to understand the past we all
                                                    choose in life
Then there would be no need for conflict anymore.

So instead of hiding behind your mask like a stick insect up a tree
Go out into your community and smile with grace
Meet all your neighbours and learn all you can
As you will be one step closer to making peace.

Sarah Fisher (15)
Lostock Hall Community High School, Preston

I Have A Dream

I have a dream that the world would be a better place,
No one would be judged on looks or race.

There would be no murder and no crime,
No one would steal, not even a dime.

People would have the courage to stand up for their rights
And hope it wouldn't cause arguments or fights.

No one would be shot dead for saying the wrong thing,
Unlike poor Martin Luther King.

If there'd be no such thing as war,
No one would get killed anymore.

Tornadoes, floods and earthquakes all cause madness,
Natural disasters make destruction and sadness.

Leanne Martland (15)
Lostock Hall Community High School, Preston

I Had A Dream

And they make a scene

There was a time,
For no crime,
The world looked creased,
For there was no crime,
At this moment in time.

This was great, only peace,
There were no thieves in sight,
Morning grew so fine,
I always thought the world was grim
And so very dim.

I hate the bullies,
They make me sad,
These bullies,
They think they are cool,
But they are fools.

Why are people cruel?
They are mean
And they make a scene.

Jordan Hall (12)
Lostock Hall Community High School, Preston

I Have A Dream

I have a dream of making the world a better place
I have a dream to save the human race
I wanna rid the streets of the crime
But to do that, I need the people to be at their prime
I have arrived because my mum and dad survived
I wanna take the gangster's guns, since they think a fly-by's fun
Now they want my skull as a prize
So I will arise
But now I have taken a gun, another war has begun
So will my dream come true?

Craig Young (14)
Lostock Hall Community High School, Preston

I Have A Dream . . .

I have a dream . . .
That no one will get judged by the colour of their skin
But by their character and all racism will stop.

I have a dream . . .
That the war in Iraq will stop
And everyone will become peaceful with each other.

I have a dream . . .
That all violence will stop and killings
And people who have killed somebody should be put in prison for life.

I have a dream . . .
That vandalism and graffiti
Children need to be kept under control
And there won't be any vandalism or graffiti.

I have a dream . . .
That all bullying will stop
And no one will get hurt.

I have a dream . . .
That the world will be a better place
With happiness all around us.

I have a dream . . .
That people won't get judged by what they do
Instead, I have a dream that they will be judged by who they are.

I have a dream . . .
That people won't steal cars, burgle other people's things
And steal from other people.

I have a dream . . .
That other people are having these dreams
And they will happen sometime.

Katie Blacklidge (12)
Lostock Hall Community High School, Preston

I Have A Dream . . .

I have a dream . . .
That bullying would stop
And people wouldn't gang up on people
Because of their appearance or problems.
I have a dream . . .
That people wouldn't get judged
By the colour of their skin
And stop getting beaten up for this
Just stop racism.
I have a dream . . .
That all the wars going on in the world
Would stop and all the nuclear weapons
Would not be used on each other
Plus stop threatening each other.
I have a dream . . .
That all the violent gangs would stop beating people up for money
And kill people to get at other people.
I have a dream . . .
That all the terrorists would stop killing innocent people
And destroying things just for no good reason.

Antony Hollinghurst (12)
Lostock Hall Community High School, Preston

Animal Cruelty

Animals shaking, hiding in fear,
Scared noises is all that you hear,
No food or water, what a dread,
Soon the poor animals will all be dead.

We carry on, just passing by,
Even if we hear the animals cry,
This is what we humans do,
This is no lie, it's honestly true.

RSPCA comes to their help,
They care about the animal's half-hearted yelp,
The animals are all caged up in sets,
One by one, they're off to the vets.

RSPCA calms the animals with soft tones,
Each one is sent off to a brand new home,
If we help the animals, like the RSPCA,
We'd make the world better, day by day.

If I had a dream,
I'd make these things come true,
Giving some money,
Is what the world should do.

Alexandra Jackson (12)
Lostock Hall Community High School, Preston

Everything

Every scar that lies on my arms
Could fill a library
Of stories and adventures
Love and hate

Every tear I have cried
Could fill a swimming pool
Children laugh and play
Never knowing how the water was made

Every drop of blood that I've made
Could fill a classroom
Of poems and pictures
All of them having a meaning

Every burn I did on purpose
Could warm up a prison cell
Jailbirds in for many reasons
I should be in there

Everything I've made or done
Could create a whole new world
Of sorrow and depression
And only on one day you're happy

Celebrate the day my world was made
Of scars, tears, blood and fire
But only one person lives here
And that is the creator of this new world.

Joanne Dixon (15)
Lostock Hall Community High School, Preston

I Had A Dream

I had a dream . . .
Of the world being a better place
No wars, no violence, no racism
Especially no bullying.

I had a dream . . .
There would be more education
More money to the fire brigades
Hospitals, police etc
Mainly those people, families
Or countries who need it most.

I had a dream . . .
That threats should stop
And laughing at people for their appearance or weight
This gives people lack of confidence.

I had a dream . . .
That the mean and nasty people in the world only bully
Because *they* have a tough life
So they take it out on everybody else
I dreamt that these bullies would go and get help in their lives.

I had a dream . . .
That you could walk past the prison cells
And most of them would be empty
And there would be no more stealing
Because it doesn't make you look big or bad.

Bethany Ashworth (11)
Lostock Hall Community High School, Preston

I Have A Dream . . .

I have a dream . . .
That when I am older I will have children
Who will grow up to be as nice and as kind as me.

I have a dream . . .
That the world would be a better place
No violence or badness.

I have a dream . . .
That everyone in the world could live forever
But that will never happen
Anything could happen though
Things that I dream could come true
If only I had a bit of thought about it.

I dream . . .
That poor people in other countries could have more food and water to
live
But only the Prime Minister and government can provide that.

I dream . . .
That when I am older I will be a professional footballer like Beckham
But only a fool would think like that.

As I dream and cry every night
Because of the tragic things that have happened in the world
I think of how the world could be a better place to live in.

I dream . . .
That I could be the Prime Minister
So I could look after the world and provide food for the poor
Also to make the world a better place.

I have a dream . . .
That I could have the courage to stand up to my enemies
But that will never happen.

I wish people wouldn't be judged
Because of the colour of their skin.

I wish all the dreams I have would come true
But I know they won't
I know that some of my dreams could come true in later life.

I have a dream . . .
I have a dream . . .
I have a dream . . .
That the world could eventually be a better place.

Darren Wiggans (13)
Lostock Hall Community High School, Preston

I Have A Dream . . .

I have a dream . . .
That world peace just happened,
People did not discriminate,
Where there is only room for those who care,
Care enough to want change for the better.

I have a dream . . .
That armies weren't needed,
Because there is no war,
That there is no disease,
No sickness, no unnecessary deaths.

I have a dream . . .
That world hunger didn't exist,
That there are no winners or losers,
That there are no leaders,
Everyone has equality.

I have a dream . . .
It will never be real,
A handful of people try to change the world,
But that isn't enough,
All we can do is dream,
But I'll never, never, never give up.

Matthew Waters (13)
Lostock Hall Community High School, Preston

I Have A Dream

Bob Geldof was having a sigh
Because of all the people that die
So he told Tony Blair
We need to send care
Or else all the people will cry.

Winston Churchill stood up
And said you should never give up
That's all he said and now he's dead
But his statement is really quite good.

Bono is a rock star
Whose words will go very far
To have the world changed
And have fun all the same
His idea is way over par.

Liam Osborn (13)
Lostock Hall Community High School, Preston

I Have A Dream . . .

I have a dream . . .
That world peace should erupt
And people would care,
Discrimination shall be stopped in its tracks
And the world shall be pure.

I have a dream . . .
Imaginations will run wild
And people will speak their minds,
Fear will not hold us back,
Instead, it shall push us forward.

I have a dream . . .
No dream is ever too small,
No dream is ever too big,
So never, never, never give up.

Lisa Taylor (13)
Lostock Hall Community High School, Preston

I Have A Dream

I have a dream . . .
That the world will be a better place
That people will be judged by the content of their character
Not by the colour of their skin
That people will never, never, never give up, to achieve their dream.

Bob Geldof has a dream
That the government will give starving people food
That the politics are spared
So it's that simple.

I have a dream . . .
That the world will be a better place
That people will be judged by the content of their character
Not by the colour of their skin
That people will never, never, never give up, to achieve their dream.

Bono is a rock star
He has the chance to do two things
To change the world
And to have fun.

I have a dream . . .
That the world will be judged by the content of their character
Not by the colour of their skin
That people will never, never, never give up, to achieve their dream.

When Ellen MacArthur was out at sea
She was never alone
There was always a team of people behind her
In her mind.

I have a dream . . .
That the world will be a better place
That people will be judged by the content of their character
Not by the colour of their skin
That people will never, never, never give up, to achieve their dream.

Jodie Renshaw (13)
Lostock Hall Community High School, Preston

I Have A Dream

I have a dream . . .
Of a better place where the world will not be judged
By colour, gender or age
But by the personality inside them
Where people never give up hope
No matter how bad the situation.

I have a dream . . .
For the world
Where it isn't about hate or greed
But for people to enjoy life
Where fears don't hold us back
From pursuing our hopes.

I have a dream . . .
For the world
That everyone can have a choice no matter what they may look like
And be able to live their dreams.

I have a dream . . .
For the world
That nobody is alone, whether in mind or body
Somebody should be there for them.

I have a dream . . .
Of freedom and justice
To help the people in need
For they are the ones that need our love most.

Matthew Evans (13)
Lostock Hall Community High School, Preston

Black-Hearted White People

Is it fair
That people stare
Scowl, spit and glare
And act like they are not there?

People are people
No matter 'bout their skin
People are people
And the colour line is thin

Why can't we live in harmony?
Is it so hard to say you are like me?
On the outside it's hard to see
Inside we're the same
In our minds we are free

People are people
No matter what
People are people
Don't matter what skin you got

What? Because you are black
You must be held back
And because you are white, you're on track,
In the know, on the map?

People are people
Remember that
A person has feelings
White or black.

Hollie McCarthy (12)
Lostock Hall Community High School, Preston

I Have A Dream . . .

I have a dream . . .
Of no poverty
No wars or arguments
I have a dream . . .
Of no pollution
No smoke or greenhouse effects
I have a dream . . .
Of no murder
No knives or gun shootings
I have a dream . . .
Of no diseases
No cancer or heart attacks
I have a dream . . .
Of no criminals
No killers or drug dealers
I have a dream . . .
Of no bad parents
No beatings no child abuse
I have a dream . . .
Of no deaths
No bombs or suicide
I have a dream . . .
Of no terrors
No floods or hurricanes
I have a dream . . .
Of a better world
But soon I will wake up.

Ellis Duncan (12)
Lostock Hall Community High School, Preston

I Have A Dream

I have a dream to live down under
To be ambitious, to stop world hunger
Racial attacks, why the need?
Help the homeless, don't beg or plead
Why the need for harmful drugs?
Hire police for mindless thugs
We should stop the pointless crime
Mindless prisoners should do more time
More and more people getting weirder
What does it take to be a world leader?
They are my dreams!

Daniel Coyne (13)
Lostock Hall Community High School, Preston

I Have A Dream

My dream is to act, to be on stage
Until I am of a very old age
I want to inspire others
Children all ages, even mothers
Not just the stage, but TV too
I want to perform in front of you
I also have another dream
To travel the world, maybe with a team
To see a cottage in the countryside
And in Australia to surf a high tide
To go to China and see the Great Wall
And New York to shop in the mall
These are my dreams and they'll stick with me
However old I will be.

Natasha Carney (11)
Montgomery High School, Blackpool

I Have A Dream

I have a dream . . .

In my dream there is no war,
No blood, no pain, no fights, no gore,
There's peace and quiet and fun and play
For happiness throughout the day.

In my dream there's no starvation,
There's health and food throughout the nation,
No death, no hurt, no pain around,
So everyone is safe and sound.

In my dream I have no fear,
No stress, no panic, throughout the year,
There's joy and laughter all around,
So everyone is safe and sound.

In my dream I heard a voice,
Who said the world could rejoice,
So people can enjoy their life,
Get rid of all the hate and strife.

As my dream comes to a close,
I know something, that no one knows,
The secret lies beneath my dream,
It's not as easy as it seems.

Katy Melling (11)
Montgomery High School, Blackpool

I Have A Dream

I have an amazing, brilliant dream
To swim in the sea so blue and clean
To breathe fresh air without the gases
To give food and water, to save the masses
To detain discrimination for a lifetime
To get rid of drugs, violence and any other crime
To stop abuse of every kind
At last, what a wonderful world we would find!

Sam Hodgson (12)
Montgomery High School, Blackpool

In My Dream

My dreams are different to my life,
I go to so many different places,
Different animals, different mountains
And so many different faces.

I have a dream there'd be world peace,
No homeless or starvation,
There wouldn't be fighting or quarrelling,
Just a quiet congregation.

I have a dream there'd be no animal cruelty,
I believe in man's best friend,
All creatures deserve their freedom
And should last until *their* end.

I have a dream there'd be no murders,
Not even petty crime,
Just to wake up in the morning,
Knowing everything's going to be fine.

My dreams are different to my life,
I go to so many different places,
Different animals, different mountains
And so many different faces.

Katie Dennett (12)
Montgomery High School, Blackpool

I Have A Dream

I have a dream as an adventurer
To travel the world and fight against the bad
That's my life
I am glad
I have a dream to stop crime
To go to court and take my time
If I stopped murder
The streets would be safer.

Jake Macrae (12)
Montgomery High School, Blackpool

I Have A Dream . . .

I have a dream . . .
It would be great if there was no war,
To travel the world and see no gore,
Conflict and war to be a thing of the past,
So people can live in harmony at last.

I have a dream . . .
If animals could live disturbance-free,
Wouldn't it be better for you and me?
To see them running wild, free to breed,
To protect their species without man's greed.

I have a dream . . .
Where the horror of pollution ends,
Protecting us from the heat the sun sends,
So the polar ice caps don't melt,
Then we're safe from what factories have dealt.

Ryan Hemming (12)
Montgomery High School, Blackpool

I Have A Dream . . .

I have a dream . . .
That the Earth was free
And joined with the sun in harmony
I have a dream . . .
That world peace will come
So the world can settle and have fun
I have a dream . . .
That drug dealers will stop
And ride up in a big bubble and pop
I have a dream . . .
That living will be free
And available to everybody
I have a dream . . .
That the sun will always shine
And life on Earth will be totally divine.

Lloyd Stevenson (11)
Montgomery High School, Blackpool

Dreaming

Thinking about the Third World countries,
The people with no food or water,
The children who lose their dad and mum,
Before they can even suck their thumb.

Listening to the harsh comments,
Aimed at people who are different,
Aimed at people with a different religion,
Wishing they could just fit in.

Watching all these wars take place,
All because of the human race,
Seeing all the men with guns,
Whilst all the public run.

So listen to me everyone,
Do as I say,
If you do,
All this madness will go away.

I am the motivator.

Follow me and help the poor,
Let's all try and stop the war,
Rise above the racist chants,
Don't listen to all the rants.

I am the motivator,
I am the inspiration.

So if you follow all these tips,
The world will not just be in bits,
The world will be whole once more
And we can live just like before.

I am the motivator,
I am the inspiration,
I am the one who can make a change.

Charlotte Raby (12)
Montgomery High School, Blackpool

I Have A Dream . . .

I have a dream . . .
To change the world,
It might be crazy, it may be absurd,
I have a dream and so do you
And one day soon, it will come true!

I have a dream . . .
To hear children's laughter,
Today, tomorrow and the day after,
Smiling faces here and there,
If smiles are here, then tears are rare.

I have a dream . . .
To swim the ocean,
While others ride in a car in motion,
Swimming far and swimming near,
It's easy if you have no fear.

I have a dream . . .
To be a great musician,
It moves you up to a new position,
Sing, drum, strum and blow,
These are useful things to know.

I have a dream . . .
To learn the law,
Listen to witnesses, hear what they saw,
If you're a criminal, best beware,
If you're not, you'd better take care.

I have a dream . . .
To change the world,
It might be crazy, it may be absurd,
I have a dream and so do you
And one day soon, it will come true!

Rebecca Sheehan (12)
Montgomery High School, Blackpool

I Have A Dream . . .

I have a dream . . .
I have a dream to have a good life
And to be a good wife
I have a dream to go to college
And to show off my knowledge

I have a dream . . .
I have a dream to make my mum and dad proud
And for me to stand out from the crowd
I have a dream to have a good job
And a rich husband called Bob

I have a dream . . .
I have a dream to walk on the moon
And I hope it will be soon
I have a dream to drive a Mini Cooper
And that would be super

Imagine . . .
Imagine a world with no stress or panic
And no death or pain
Imagine a world where everyone's safe
And there's no blood or gore

Imagine . . .
Imagine a world with poverty gone
And no war
Imagine a world with laughter and joy
That's my world

Do you have a dream?

Emma Wainwright (12)
Montgomery High School, Blackpool

Inspired

The look upon a child's face
Their gratitude
Just because of the simple things we bring
Like water and food

When soldiers fight for solidarity
When peace spreads through the world
When enemies unite as one
And stand so very bold

People so frail and scared
Wires all around
Trying to fight this evil curse
New cures needing to be found

I will try to follow in your footsteps
You are my inspiration
You will guide me
You are the path, I am the determination

When people's faces light up with thanks
When it's you who made them smile
With everyone as a whole
This feeling will last a very long while

Never any problems
No racist remarks, no threats, no tears
All our worries are shared
Everyone is equal, without fears.

Ashleigh Good (12)
Montgomery High School, Blackpool

I Have A Dream . . .

I have a dream . . .
White sandy beaches,
Posh, expensive bars,
Designer shoes and dresses
And fast, flashy cars.
I have a dream . . .
Big, fancy houses,
Huge diamond rings,
Massive, strong bouncers,
I wish I had those things.
I have a dream . . .
Saunas and steam rooms,
A widescreen TV,
Jacuzzis and a swimming pool,
Their life is so easy.
I have a dream . . .
Paris to Rome,
Huge, ravin' clubs,
Fashionable jewellery
And bubbling hot tubs.
I have a dream . . .
I don't want a lot,
But to be a celeb
And I want my dream to start,
When I go to bed.

Shannon Rees (12)
Montgomery High School, Blackpool

I Have A Dream

I have a dream,
An inspiration,
No more frustration,
In this world.

Everyone at peace,
The wars are no more,
The rich and the poor,
Are treated equally.

I have a dream,
An inspiration,
No more frustration,
In this world.

Food and water is available everywhere,
No one shall starve or die of thirst,
All our bad ways are reversed,
Everyone is happy.

I have a dream,
An inspiration,
No more frustration,
In this world.

All the countries,
Treated like one,
Everyone shall have such fun,
Playing together.

I have a dream,
So follow me,
Together we have the key
To make things better.

Holly Wadeson (12)
Montgomery High School, Blackpool

I Have A Dream

I have a dream
That poachers will cease
To shoot defenceless animals

The monkey
The chimpanzee
And the gorilla with its mighty chest

The ferocious lion
To the laughing hyena
All started off as precious cubs

The circus to free its animals
Into the open wild

Stop the juggling
Plate spinning
And acrobatics

Elephants in tutus
No, it should not be
They should be in the jungle
Eating off the trees

More nature reserves are needed
Our animals aren't safe
In the world
There are no boundaries

Freedom is everywhere
Lakes and waterfalls
Fruit all around

I have a dream
For animals
To be *free!*

Aidan Radcliffe (12)
Montgomery High School, Blackpool

I Have A Dream

I have a dream that people could walk down the street
Without the fear of being beat
That people had more food and water
That parents didn't abuse their sons or daughters
That people lived in harmony
That innocent people were let free
Murderers got deported
People stood up, people got reported
Stand up for the things that are right
Trying with all your might
I have a dream

People could walk down the street
Without fear of being beat
Stylish clothes weren't an issue
People didn't just throw their tissues
Blacks and whites could live together
No more racial deaths forever
I have a dream.

Joshua Barrow (12)
Montgomery High School, Blackpool

I Have A Dream

I have a dream to cure a cold
I have a dream to cure the old

I have a dream to cure a cat
I have a dream to cure a rat

I have a dream to cure all sneezes
I have a dream to cure all wheezes

I have a dream to stop racist words
So all the abuse can't be heard

And if all this came true
I would be able to help you.

Jack McFarlane (12)
Montgomery High School, Blackpool

I Have A Dream

I have a dream . . .
That war would cease
I have a dream . . .
That everywhere had peace
I have a dream . . .
That we were one
I have a dream . . .
That racism was gone
I have a dream . . .
That all bullying was sorted
I have a dream . . .
That war missions were aborted
I have a dream . . .
That all this would come true
So that the world would be better
For me and you
I have a dream.

Becky Hoddinott (12)
Montgomery High School, Blackpool

I Have A Dream

For me
I have a dream to be a footballer
Play for England and Liverpool
And earn a lot of money

For children
To have a good life
To be very happy as the sun
For them to have good jobs.

For everyone
Racism to stop altogether
No bombings in the whole world
And for them to have a good life.

Louise Latham (12)
Montgomery High School, Blackpool

A Dream To Change The World

I have a dream to change the world
To stop the wars and fights
Motivation, inspiration
Will destroy these awful sights

I have a dream to change the world
That black and white will mix
To treat each other equally
To mend this racist fix

I have a dream to change the world
To stop polluting air
Stop throwing litter on the floor
And act as if we care

I have a dream to change the world
For people old and new
To bring peace to everyone
I hope my dream comes true.

Hollie Rigby (12)
Montgomery High School, Blackpool

I Have A Dream

I have a dream
To be a surfer,
Wind blowing through my hair,
But I have another dream,
World peace,
A world where racists don't exist,
Where children can play safely.

Every day filled with happiness,
For people all over the world,
Poverty - it won't exist,
Every child, a nice warm bed,
I have a dream
But I hope both will come true.

Naomi Gilby (12)
Montgomery High School, Blackpool

I Have A Dream

I have a dream
Not to be slowly killed
By the black cloud hanging above me
But will this dream ever be fulfilled?

To play in the rain
And sit on the sand
Breath fresh air
Hold Mother Nature's hand.

I wish this radiation
Would go away
Step out of the microwave
Come out and play!

But this dream
Can never be
My home will always be poisoned
So will my blood, the sand and the sea.

The reactor - why did it blow?
Take my daddy, his colleagues, his factory
The town around - why did they go?
My mates, my school, they all went then.

I want them all back
My life, my fresh air
My dad, my home
The death zone not there.

I must say goodbye
To all of these things
I'll never have my life back
But still, a girl can dream.

Rebecca Davies (12)
Montgomery High School, Blackpool

I Have A Dream

I have a dream,
In an ideal world,
That abuse wouldn't happen,
To young boys and girls.

Shaking with fear,
Cries and moans,
Why should these children suffer
In their own home

Let's find a way
To take away their pain
And make their lives
Seem normal again.

I have a dream,
In an ideal world,
That abuse wouldn't happen,
To young boys and girls.

Rebecca Mills (11)
Montgomery High School, Blackpool

I Have A Dream

To see one's love in one's eyes,
See birds flying in the skies,
To find the meaning of our lives,
No one in violence using knives.

I want all the poverty to stop,
I want to see the world at its top,
Why can't everyone just be friends?
Not driving people round the bend.

I have a dream,
I like to imagine,
These are my thoughts,
Of the world.

I wish,
Someone would,
Listen to me now,
Before it's too late.

Catherine Pullen (12)
Montgomery High School, Blackpool

I Have A Dream

I have a dream to be ace at drawing
To be able to draw the start of morning
To be able to draw the moon in the night
To be able to draw a man in a fight
I want to draw the Eiffel Tower
I want to draw the clock in an hour
I want to draw the wonders of the town
I want to draw someone's frown
To be able to draw a rack of bones
To be able to draw a line of phones
To be able to draw the pictures for a book
To be able to draw Captain Hook's hook
To be able to draw the designs for a house
To be able to draw the whiskers of a mouse
I have a dream to be ace at drawing
To be able to dream the start of morning.

Luke Cable (12)
Montgomery High School, Blackpool

I Have A Dream

For me
To meet Neyo, to hear him sing live
He is so sweet, he makes me dream
He makes me dream!

For children
To have happiness
To have love
To have peace
To have a caring family!

For everyone
Everyone needs a family
Everyone needs love
Everyone needs a home
So everyone needs a hug!

Chenice Kiernan (12)
Montgomery High School, Blackpool

I Have A Dream . . .

I have a dream . . .
That the world is full of happiness
A dream that is full of hope
People looking after one another, caring and sharing
Helping everyone in the world.

I have a dream . . .
That all the children in the world care for each other
That all the children with no homes stay alive
And get provided with food and schools and buildings
I have a dream that all the children are happy.

I have a dream that everyone is full of love
And that everyone is loving and caring
That the whole world cares for each other
I have a dream that the world is better.

Laura Walmsley (12)
Montgomery High School, Blackpool

I Have A Dream

Money for the rich,
Money for the poor,
Money rolling on the floor.
Money for the old,
Money for the new,
Money for a small man living in a shoe.
Money for a game,
Money for a watch,
Money for a small, tatty matchbox.
Money for a car,
Money for a plane,
Money for a ticket to sunny, sunny Spain.
Money not for all,
Money just for some,
Money for the work of an old man's son.

Thomas Roy Hornsby (12)
Montgomery High School, Blackpool

I Had A Dream

I had a dream,
I was famous,
Everyone knew me,
I was in all the papers.

I had a dream,
That I was a fantastic musician,
Everyone listened to my music,
Everyone played it.

I had a dream,
That I was a chef,
People travelled all over the world
To taste my food.

I had a dream,
That I was an artist,
I painted pictures that were sold
All over the world.

I had a dream,
That I had plenty of cash,
Everyone knew me, everyone loved me,
Then I woke up, oh well!

Louis Garrick (12)
Montgomery High School, Blackpool

I Have A Dream . . .

I have a dream . . .
That the world will be a better place
Get rid of all the nasty race
Carry on the good education
Get rid of all the bad temptations.

I have a dream . . .
That the poor will get a better life
Get rid of all the people's strife
To send the poor people what they want
Instead, just try, don't say you can't.

I have a dream . . .
That the world will come together
And let us all live a happy life forever
To give us a chance to apologise
And let all the goodness rise.

I have a dream . . .
That I can help make all these changes
Change all different things and all sorts of ranges
To the top of mountains, to the bottom of the sea
To help everybody, not just you and me!

Rachel Bullock (12)
Montgomery High School, Blackpool

I Have A Dream . . .

I have a dream . . .
A world with no violence
Where everything's calm
With no horrid people causing harm

I have a dream . . .
Of flowers growing everywhere
None of them being stood on
Then people will stop and stare

I have a dream . . .
Of people being kind to one another
No fights in pubs and bars
If this carries on, we'll go to Mars

I have a dream . . .
Of fresh fruit and veg
Being grown every day
And horses lying on fresh hay.

Bethany Spooner (12)
Montgomery High School, Blackpool

I Have A Dream

Perhaps your dream is short and sweet,
But for me, I can say, it is rather more deep,
I don't intend to brag, nor either to boast,
For this passion inside me, is what matters the most.

A loyal heart and inspiration is all you need,
To banish all prejudice on colour and creed,
No matter who you are, or who you love,
You'll always have a blessing from those above.

If you have determination and a heart of gold,
Listen to the music, turn away from the cold,
You know you can do it, come on, persevere,
Think of the children, their lives not so clear.

If I can't persuade you, think of world hunger,
If we all stick together, we can help them live longer,
I know you can do it, come and join me,
For a world free of poverty and tragedy.

Stephanie Rawlinson (12)
Montgomery High School, Blackpool

I Have A Dream

For me I have a dream
To be forever dancing
Going up and down the stage, prancing
Twizzling and twirling around and around
Beating to the fastest sound
For me to be simply the best.

For children in Africa
That they have water, food, parents and shelter
And so they can go on a helter-skelter
So they can have love from above
For evermore they can go on and live.

For everyone to have a dream to be happy
So they can have peace
And they can go on the lease
They can be happy and have peace
No war, no heartbreak
No one dies and no families are destroyed.

Ellie May Austin (12)
Montgomery High School, Blackpool

I Have A Dream . . .

I have a dream . . .
That the world could be a better place for you and me to live,
No conflict, no friendship broken,
Just peace.

I have a dream . . .
That there were cures for every illness,
No suffering, no dying painfully,
Just peace.

I have a dream . . .
That natural disasters didn't happen,
No homes destroyed, no families lost,
Just peace.

I have a dream . . .
That only good things happen,
No bad in people's hearts, no enemies,
Just peace.

I wish.

Lauren Oatley (12)
Montgomery High School, Blackpool

I Have A Dream . . .

I have a dream . . .
That is full of happiness
I have a dream . . .
That is full of hope
Loving and giving is also a dream
Caring and helping with serious diseases
Helping everybody

I have a dream . . .
That children will be great
Especially Nicole, AAliyah, Rhianna, Robbie and Megan
Running around like troops in a battle
Crying and sleeping is all they do

I have a dream . . .
That is full of love
I have a dream . . .
That is full of life
Everyone shopping for clothes and food
Pleasing and teasing is great for everyone
I have a dream.

Emma Pilkington (12)
Montgomery High School, Blackpool

I Have A Dream . . .

I have a dream . . .
That England won the World Cup this year
The triumph of it is so near
It would be great if we won
It would be, oh, so much fun!

I have a dream . . .
That all countries meet as one
Sharing talent, tackles, the ball is won
Exciting, thrilling, enjoying the game
Goals, fans cheering players' names.

I have a dream . . .
Flags waving, colours red and white
England's glory, pride and players' might
As they bring home the great World Cup
Beckham and the team stand up.

I have a dream . . .
The World Cup is brought home
And all along I have known
Just how great the players are
The nation sings, near and far.

William Hirst (12)
Montgomery High School, Blackpool

I Have A Dream

I have a dream,
That has a theme,
That theme is football,
My dream will never fall.

I want to be a pro someday,
It doesn't matter about the pay,
I'll play for fun
And when I play, I run, run, *run!*

I love the game,
Every match is never the same,
Every match a goal is scored,
How can you ever get bored?

My hero is Rooney,
Even though he looks a bit gooney,
I also like David Beckham
And with his skills, we're gonna beat 'em.

In Germany this year,
We'll drink all their beer,
We'll just shout and shout,
Till we all pass out.

Maybe I'll play in the cup soon,
Eight years from June,
My dream is football,
That is all.

Jordan Grenaghan (12)
Montgomery High School, Blackpool

I Have A Dream . . .

I have a dream . . .
For England to win,
Every match they play,
To score the goal for the World Cup.

I have a dream . . .
Brazil will lose,
England will win,
Glory all around.

I have a dream . . .
That England win on penalties,
The whole of England go crazy,
The Mexican wave goes round.

I have a dream . . .
Beckham to swerve the ball,
In the net
And the crowd to roar.

I have a dream . . .
For Owen to run in and out of the players,
One by one, they all go down,
Bang! 3-0 to England.

I have a dream . . .
For Robinson to save the last penalty,
To dive in the air,
But then again, it's only a dream.

Shannon Quilligan (12)
Montgomery High School, Blackpool

Football Dream

I have a dream . . .
To be a footballer
I would be as fast as a cheetah
To the fans, I would be a king
Signing autographs is an annoying thing

I have a dream . . .
I would play for Manchester United
Before the match, I would get excited
My wife's closet is a shop
When I get injured, I have to hop off

I have a dream . . .
In my spare time I play with my son
Or go down to the pub
Playing football is the best thing
So just call me the king
That's my dream.

Eric Clayton (12)
Montgomery High School, Blackpool

I Had A Dream

I had a dream
That I won the lottery
Hip hip hooray
If I won the lottery
I would spend all day
If I won the lottery
Clothes, shoes, everything coming my way
If I won the lottery
I would shop all day
If I won the lottery
I would be happy all the way
If I won the lottery
I would put some in my bank
That's what I will do
If I win the lottery.

Hollie Wolstencroft (12)
Montgomery High School, Blackpool

I Have A Dream . . .

I have a dream . . .
Where everything is safe
And everywhere you go everybody has faith
There's lots of animals playing all around
If you want to speak, don't shout out loud

I have a dream . . .
Where children are not starving
But instead the children will start laughing
No child or baby will be abused
Because all the abusers will be accused

I have a dream . . .
There are no more wars
And everybody follows the laws
Just follow the laws the judge suggested
Then there will be no need to be arrested.

Nicole Snelson (12)
Montgomery High School, Blackpool

I Have A Dream . . .

I have a dream . . .
To be a dancer
To dance on the glittery floor
As I dance through the door
People applaud.

I have a dream . . .
For children who need love
We don't want them to go up above
They can be so sweet
If you give them a treat.

I have a dream . . .
That all homeless people get a home
So they don't live on the street
They can be so sweet
If you give them somewhere to sleep.

Danielle Phillips (12)
Montgomery High School, Blackpool

I Have A Dream

I have a dream,
It'll make your faces beam,
England will win the World Cup,
That will cheer us all up.

Gerrard will score a magnificent goal,
They'll all drop out down a big black hole,
Rooney will be fit enough to play,
So we'll be singing all the way.

Robinson will save all the shots,
He'll be rewarded lots and lots,
Paraguay and Sweden are going down,
We'll be jogging through the town.

Lampard will header one in,
Rubbish players in the sin bin,
Beckham will take a brilliant free kick,
Round the wall, curling quick.

Liam Wolstencroft (12)
Montgomery High School, Blackpool

World Cup

I had a dream,
About my team,
Beckham running with the ball,
England fans loudly call,
'Come on Becks, you're the cream,
Finest of the football team,'
Beckham shoots, the ball goes high,
Rising up into the sky,
Crouch is waiting, heads it in,
The crowd explodes in a mighty din,
At the centre they begin,
Every player wants to win,
Now it's Gerrard on the ball,
Their defence is like a wall,
Then a gap and Owen's there,
He flicks the ball with the greatest care,
The whistle goes, the game is done,
The England team have won, won, *won!*

Michael Phillips (12)
Montgomery High School, Blackpool

I Have A Dream . . .

I have a dream . . .
To be an RAF pilot,
To let my plane gleam,
It would impress my lot,
I have a dream.

I have a dream . . .
To dodge enemy firing,
To fly over troops in a stream
And it doesn't get tiring,
I have a dream.

I have a dream . . .
To fly F14 Tomcats,
To go so fast, I look like a light beam,
That every time I land, the ground is flat,
I have a dream.

I have a dream . . .
To serve my country,
To work as a team,
To force terrorists out of my country,
I have a dream . . .
. . . I have a dream.

Luke Brisco (12)
Montgomery High School, Blackpool

I Have A Dream

To feel the wind blow through my hair,
I ride the carousel at the fair,
It sweeps me along as if on a cloud,
I'm so full of joy, I scream aloud.

To see baby animals play on a farm,
Their grazing parents sitting quiet and calm,
I swim with the fish in the sea,
I'm feeding them bread for their tea.

To hear a small tweeting bird,
All is silent, no one speaks a word,
My little sister screams and shouts,
My mum goes in to bawl her out.

To smell the fresh cheddar cheese,
I ask my dad, 'Can I have some please?'
The sun has gone down, the candles are lit,
Alone in my room, here I sit.

To taste fresh strawberries that I've just picked,
Through pages of a recipe book, I flicked,
What a strange world it does seem,
Looking at it from my dream.

Melanie Kane (12)
Montgomery High School, Blackpool

I Have A Dream . . .

I have a dream . . .
A dream to become a pop singer,
A dream to become a star,
A dream to save the animals,
A dream to work on Mars.

A dream to save the dying,
A dream to save the world,
A dream to stop global warming,
To stop pollution and litter getting hurled.

A dream to stop poverty,
A dream to help the poor,
A dream to help the hurt,
The handicapped, the disabled and the sore.

So if this is too much to ask,
Think yourself lucky,
That you can read this poem
In the comfort of your homes, cars and schools,
Something unheard of in some people's lives.

Adam McKay (12)
Montgomery High School, Blackpool

I Have A Dream . . .

I have a dream . . .
That I could be an engineer, the best in the world,
Nice, so kind and safe,
This is my dream.

I have a dream . . .
That children could be looked after in the world,
No ill children,
This is my dream.

I have a dream . . .
That war would finish in the world,
No dying, all living,
This is my dream.

If these dreams come true
The world will be a wonderful place
No pain, just peace and being calm
These are my dreams.

These are my dreams
And they will never change.

Joshua Connolly (12)
Montgomery High School, Blackpool

I Have A Dream

I have a dream
Of love at first sight
I am a princess
He is the knight

You meet the one
Your heart beats wild
He calls your name
His voice so tender and mild

He asks you out
You jump for joy
You tell your friends,
'I love this boy'

We go on a date
Acting so shy
We loved our meals
We shared apple pie

He takes you home
You invite him in
Your first real kiss
It's not a sin.

Olivia Pennington (12)
Montgomery High School, Blackpool

I Have A Dream

I have a dream
About going into space
Seeing all the planets
Landing on Mars
Looking at Earth
Eating space food
And flying all around.

Zooming in a rocket
In and out of planets
Feeling which is coldest
Feeling which is warmest
Seeing inside a spaceship
Pushing every button
Seeing which one works.

Slowly going back to Earth
Taking one last glance
Saying which one I like most
Entered Earth and going flat out
Soon I'll be at the ground
Reached the stand
And got locked up.

Craig Tordoff (12)
Montgomery High School, Blackpool

I Have A Dream

I have a dream to reach for the stars
I might even reach Mars
Shooting through the Milky Way
Maybe see some aliens on the way.

Walking across the moon
Digging my feet in like a spoon
Eating the planet on my knees
It surely is made of cheese.

Seeing the rocket ships pass me by
I'm so glad I can fly
Doing the famous spaceman bounce
There's no gravity, I don't weigh an ounce.

I'm glad my dream has come true
I wish you could have come too
To see the views of the outer space
It's a wonderful, magical, beautiful place.

April Shillingford (12)
Montgomery High School, Blackpool

I Have A Dream

For me . . .
I have a dream to become a dancer,
To entertain the world,
I will twirl and I will swirl
And I'll dance and I'll prance
Across the stage floor
My shiny and glittery costume
Will glisten and shine in the lights.

For children . . .
I have a dream for children to have
A happy and a joyful life
With a good job.

For everyone . . .
I have a dream for everyone not to starve
And to have a good and happy life
As well as a good job
With no bombings or starvation in this world.

Sarah Lomax (12)
Montgomery High School, Blackpool

I Have A Dream . . .

I have a dream . . .
For people to stop being racist,
For white people to like coloured,
For us to accept them in our world.

I have a dream . . .
That people will care for each other,
No matter their colour,
For us to help them when they're hurt.

I have a dream . . .
A dream to help,
Families that feel pressured by a different colour,
For the coloured to like the white.

I have a dream . . .
That children can be happy,
No matter what their colour
And not get bullied.

I have a dream . . .
For white not to bully the coloured
And for them to not bully white
For them to get along and be happy.

I have a dream . . .
For managers to accept all coloured people,
For them not to be racist,
I have a dream . . .
I have a dream!

Aimee Booth (12)
Montgomery High School, Blackpool

I Have A Dream . . .

I have a dream . . .
To be able to fly
High as a bird in the sky
Flying through clouds
Shooting past planes
And looking down at people rushing about.

I have a dream . . .
To become a scientist
To cure every sickness
From a cold to cancer
It'll be gone with a wink of an eye.

I have a dream . . .
To help people in poor countries
To give them money
To get food and water.

I have a dream . . .
To control all teachers
To get them to have
The funniest lesson ever
To let us play games
And just talk all day
And when they tell you to stop running in the corridor
You would just make them go back to their lessons.

I have a dream . . .
To be able to get rid of all boring things
And replace them with all cool things.

Reece Brown (12)
Montgomery High School, Blackpool

I Have A Dream . . .

I have a dream . . .
A dream no one would ever seem
A dream that I lived next to a stream
And that's my dream.

I lived in a nice big house
Quiet, with no people about
And that's a good dream
I'd go swimming in my stream.

I have a dream . . .
Of a magical place
Beyond time and space
Where love and affection
Existed for the human race.

I have a dream . . .
To be the best
I have a dream . . .
To beat the rest
And that's my dream.

Joe Willman (12)
Montgomery High School, Blackpool

If Only . . .

If only the pain flooding into our lives
Washed away,
If only the world learnt to listen,
A new day,
Perhaps we would find it in our hearts
To stop the hate and violence
And instead of painful screams,
We would only hear golden silence,
The idea floats around all the time
But not all people believe,
Maybe, in the future, all will be well,
It's not too hard to perceive.

Andy Boardman (12)
SS Peter & Paul RC High School (Lower), Widnes

Liberation Lives

Grant the children their freedom,
Let them lead their normal lives,
Sweep your hand over their childhood,
Remove the terror, evil, lies.

Fight your fear of failure,
Your desperate need to succeed,
Lose your over-grown ego,
Clear your eyes so you can see.

Liberate their fighting existence,
Realise their great need,
Return their feelings of security,
Give them a new life to lead.

Show them a way to abolish their hatred,
Fill the gap with joy and peace,
Give them a gift of love so strong,
Which is sure to never cease.

Jessica Grainger (13)
SS Peter & Paul RC High School (Lower), Widnes

Why Go To War?

W hat is the point?
H ow can you live with killing
Y our fellow humans?

G uns and swords, tanks and bombs
O r what about a hand grenade?

T hink of all the people who lose families
O r what about the families of those people?

W hen Bush and Blair say so
A ll the men fight, but is there a
R eason for this?

Emily Shaw (13)
St Aidan's CE High School, Poulton-le-Fylde

I Have A Dream . . .

I have a dream . . .
That all the different races
Will come together as friends
And work as a team
I have a dream . . .
That all wars will come to an end
I have a dream . . .
That people will come together as one
I have a dream . . .
That people will be judged
By what they are inside
Not what they appear to be
I have a dream . . .
That all my dreams
Will one day
Come true.

Chris Williamson (13)
St Aidan's CE High School, Poulton-le-Fylde

I Have A Dream

I don't lead a great life
But I have a dream that everything will be alright
Time goes swiftly on its way
All too soon we've lost today
Make the most of your time
Because soon you will see life is tough

So I have a dream that people will lead good lives
I have a dream that racism, prejudice and discrimination
                                    will no longer exist
I have a dream that enemies will come together as friends
I have a dream that our world will be good

Follow your dream and give it your best
Soon,
You will find success.

Abbie Ronson (13)
St Aidan's CE High School, Poulton-le-Fylde

A Third World

People queuing up outside McDonald's,
Filling up with processed meat,
Greasy chips, artificial nuggets,
Four thousand calories a day.

Think of all the people in the Third World countries,
Starving so their ribs show,
Five people dying every minute,
One hundred calories a day.

Gulping down fizzy drinks,
Lemonade and Coke,
All those additives being consumed,
Four thousand calories a day.

Africans walking miles for water,
Across the dirt and sand,
Mothers holding their babies,
Watching them die,
From starvation, dehydration.

God provides, Man decides.

Rachel Oliver (13)
St Aidan's CE High School, Poulton-le-Fylde

My Dream

I have a dream . . .
A dream that the world will bind together as one,
A dream that everyone is treated equally,
A dream of freedom,
A dream of caring citizens,
A dream where people can be who they want to be,
A dream that when people are hungry, they are fed,
A dream that everybody has someone to turn to,
Who can make my dream come true?
You!

Verity Corbett (13)
St Aidan's CE High School, Poulton-le-Fylde

I Have A Dream!

My dream is to win the lottery
Money, big amounts or small

I have a dream!

Poor Africans have a dream to be clean
To have a taste of our lifestyle

They have a dream!

You want happiness in life
Being yourself, an individual

You have a dream!

We want world peace
All races living together as families
No violence

We have a dream!

Millions of dreams dreamt each night
All different

The world has a dream!

Jessica Aspinall (13)
St Aidan's CE High School, Poulton-le-Fylde

I Had A Dream

I had a dream, that all people throughout the world
Were treated as equals
Banish poverty
Stop starvation
Make racism history
Respect the disabled needs
We were all born as people
Greed and inhumanity is taking over
Let's do something about it
And make sure this does not remain as a dream.

Alice Jones (13)
St Aidan's CE High School, Poulton-le-Fylde

I Have A Dream

I have a dream
A dream of the future

When the environment will be appreciated,
The trees, the birds, the flowers and the animals.

I have a dream
A dream of the future

When the good in people will shine over
The bad within

I have a dream
A dream of tomorrow

When war and conflict will be crushed,
And where there will be peace

I have a dream

I have a dream

A dream for the future.

Dominic Hale (12)
St Aidan's CE High School, Poulton-le-Fylde

I Have A Dream

Hopes and fears
No more tears
Why is there war?
What is if for?

End the suffering
And the loss of life
Help every husband
Come home to his family and wife.

Help keep the peace and divide us none
Each colour, race and religion live as one
Stop the fighting!
Let us unite!

Laura Thistleton (13)
St Aidan's CE High School, Poulton-le-Fylde

I Have A Dream . . .

I have a dream . . .
That there will be no fighting,
That different religions
Could stand together as one
Without violence.

I have a dream . . .
That when I grow up,
I'll be safer
On the streets of Britain.

I have a dream . . .
That when my children grow up,
I will not be worried,
About drugs, thieves or even murderers.

I have a dream . . .
That scientists will find,
A cure for cancer
And save thousands of people.

We have a dream . . .
That together, one and all,
Can make our dreams,
Come true and save thousands of lives.

One world,
Thousands of dreams!

Meghan Clarkson (13)
St Aidan's CE High School, Poulton-le-Fylde

I Have A Dream . . .

I have a dream . . .
That I can live
Knowing that the grass is green
And the sky is blue
And everything is even
With no obstacles in my happy life.

I have a dream . . .
That people will
Never, never, never give up
People will persist until they triumph
Good will prevail over the bad.

I have a dream . . .
That people will be able to see
What they are doing wrong
We shall change
We need to change
If the world is to stay as it is.

I have a dream . . .
That people will always
Have someone to support them
Through thick and thin
They will work as a team
And so will our children.

I have a dream . . .
That peace will be in all of us
Yes, we need enemies
But we don't need to fight and squabble
God made us better than that.

I have a dream . . .

Sam Eastick (12)
St Aidan's CE High School, Poulton-le-Fylde

Stay True To Pink

Singer, songwriter,
Her music inspires thousands every day,
Performing artist,
Winning in every possible way.

Childhood traumas:
Crying into her pillow, feeling alone,
Walking by herself,
Running away from everything she called home.

Growing up is hard,
Parents splitting up, families driven apart,
Beating the bullies,
Piecing together her broken heart.

Now she has moved one,
A new name, a new person, a new life,
Alecia Moore, now Pink,
Helping many others with songs of her strife.

Now I can see that,
We are born unique and so we should stay
No matter what
Remain true to yourself, come what may.

Sophie Large (13)
St Aidan's CE High School, Poulton-le-Fylde

I Have A Dream

I have a dream that;
One day people all over the world,
Will treat and respect everyone equally;
As we are one race - the human race.

Black or white; old or young;
Boy or girl; Catholic or Christian;
Hard-working or lazy; quiet or loud;
Good example or one to ignore;
Friend or enemy;
My dream is that one day we will all;
Respect and be friends with everyone.

I have a dream that everyone will have a good life,
No disabilities and no other problems,
No unhappy people and no suicide,
No bombings, no cruelty and no war.

I have a dream that every human will know
Their right to be on Earth,
No one will be left out
And Earth's motto will be;
Peace, love and friendship.

My dream is for harmonious equality on Earth.

My inspiration is partly Martin Luther King
In the case of difference races on Earth
But these are my thoughts and wishes.

Adam Harrisson (13)
St Aidan's CE High School, Poulton-le-Fylde

I Have A Dream

I have a dream,
A dream just for me,
A dream that inspires
And that's perfect for me.

You have a dream,
A dream just for you,
A dream that inspires,
A dream special to you.

But who inspires our dreams?
Who appears and helps us on?
Someone famous or no one at all,
Comes again to lead you on.

That person's special to you
And is different for everyone,
They inspire and encourage,
To each and every one.

I have a dream,
A dream just for me,
A dream that inspires
And that's perfect for me.

Claire Sycamore (13)
St Aidan's CE High School, Poulton-le-Fylde

I Have A Dream

You may say I am deluded,
That recycling is such a bore!
But very soon another tree,
Will come tumbling to the floor.

They won't be here forever,
So preserve them while you can,
Recycle your spare cans and card,
Repair the damage done by man!

Charlotte Mallinson (13)
St Aidan's CE High School, Poulton-le-Fylde

I Have A Dream

Surely it is not fair,
That people can't breathe the same air,
That people can't board the same trains,
Or even walk past the same drains.

Maybe some time in the future,
People will share the same tutor,
No matter what our colour or creed,
No matter what colour blood we bleed.

Maybe people will understand,
That racist tactics are underhand,
We are all equal in rights,
There is no need to start fights.

The riots and fighting must end,
To each other, a hand we must lend,
A peaceful solution should be found,
So that people are equal, the whole world around.

David Walsh (13)
St Aidan's CE High School, Poulton-le-Fylde

Dreams

My dream is to drive a Swedish car
My dream is to be rich with a Hummer
My dream is to ride a Yamaha R1
My dream is to have a big house with three motorbikes and three cars
My dream is to be King of England
My dream is to have a property abroad
My dream is to be a comedian
My dream is to go on holiday to Brazil
My dream is to be a Brazilian dancer
My dream is to own a yacht
My dream is to be a builder
My dream is to be a good husband and a good father.

Corey Leon Jolliffe (13)
Summerseat Residential School, Bury

I Have A Dream

My dream is to become a traveller to see the world's delights,
Visit Cairo's tombs and pyramids and catch a fright,
I decided to go to Australia to see something new,
After a week I got into a fight with a kangaroo,
I then went to the North Pole,
But unfortunately I slipped and landed in a hole,
After a look around there wasn't any sights,
So I sat down and watched the Northern Lights,
I set off to Cuba
And on my boat was a man playing the tuba,
When I got to Cuba I smoked my first cigar,
Then I realised my lungs will be full of tar,
I decided to travel south to Brazil and watched their famous football
team,
After the match I had a scream,
My last stop was Saudi Arabia a land full of oil,
Now I have finished my long journey, I am back to British soil,
I rose like the sun and released lots of shine,
Maybe when I go to bed and lie,
I will travel to the sky.

Adrian Kirkwilliam (15)
Summerseat Residential School, Bury

I Had A Dream

I had a dream
It came like a bright, shining beam!
In my dream,
I'm like a cat with the cream!
And you are supreme!

Antony Mahon (13)
Summerseat Residential School, Bury

I Have A Dream

My dream is to travel
And see all the sights.
The world is my oyster
I'll marvel in delight.

In Rome I'd eat pizza
And stroll round the ruins
Maybe find treasure.

Experience culture in France
Savour all the wine
Taste frogs' legs and snails.

In Egypt view the pyramids
Marvel at the mummies
Search for the king known as Tutankhamen.

Next to Australia with a didgeridoo, kangaroos
Wallabies, boomerangs too
I'll see the sights
And see the world.

Off to Jamaica to see Bob Marley
Went to America
Saw the President.

But I won't see the sights
And I won't see the world
Because I woke in my bed
It was all a dream
My dream.

Simon Smith (15)
Summerseat Residential School, Bury

I Have A Dream

My dream would be to rule the world
There would be no rules,
Except no stealing and no education.

No one would dare of thinking of messing with me
I would rule the world . . .

That would be my dream
I would own Jamaica, selling the biggest and best
Natural high . . .

I would be known throughout the world
I would be a gangster having my own tiger
And my own selection of cars . . .

From New York to Spain,
North Pole to South . . .
Everything would be mine . . .

That's my *dream* . . .

Mike Whitnall (15)
Summerseat Residential School, Bury

I Had A Dream

I had a dream
The rain falls from the sky
So high
Then you can have a swim
You can eat honey
Honey looks like gold balls
Your dream feels so good
Then you can feel yourself flying
Your sister has a dream too
In your dream you feel so scared
And you feel yourself shaking
You wake up in the night
You smell so good.

Lisa Bland (14)
Summerseat Residential School, Bury

I Have A Dream

I have a dream that one day
All my troubles will decay
Walk the street as light as a spirit

I visit my loved ones
In the background there are love songs
My friends and family playing on my feelings

A tear in my mother's eye
I'm screaming my loudest, 'Please don't cry.'
Why doesn't she hear me?

A golden shine in the clouds
There were just smiles, no frowns
That was the last thing I remember

Now it's time to say goodbye
Open my wings and away I fly
To spend the rest of time over my loved ones.

Daniel Bates (16)
Summerseat Residential School, Bury

I Have A Dream

My dream is money
I'll have all the honeys
My bank account is full
Walk down the street and pull

A life of luxury for me
My mansion at the side of the sea
Abroad in Spain
Where there's no rain

My business is large
I'm the man in charge
My wage is unbelievable
With money, anything is achievable.

Ashli Charnock (15)
Summerseat Residential School, Bury

I Have A Dream . . .

I have a dream . . .
That there will be no school
And more pubs for the ages of 14 to 18

I have a dream . . .
That young people will be allowed
To drive cars, motorbikes, quads on the streets

I have a dream . . .
That there will be more fishing areas
And more funfairs

I have a dream . . .
That all the violence will stop
And all the killing will stop too

I have a dream . . .
That the government
Will think of younger people

I have a dream . . .
That young people can grow up
With a world that is safe and secure.

Tom Weatherilt (15)
Summerseat Residential School, Bury

My Dreams

M is for money, I want loads when I grow up
Y is for Yankees, play in the Superbowl Cup

D is for dangerous, the wildlife in Brazil
R is for roller coaster, just for the thrill
E is for England, play against the world
A is for amazing, into the top corner it curled
M is for monkey, and pandas as well
S is for saving, saving species that would be swell.

Ben Holmes (13)
Summerseat Residential School, Bury

If I Had A Dream

I would be friends with everyone
I would fly
Nothing would weigh over a ton
No one would die.

If I had a dream
I would have money every day
No one would be rich or poor
I would never get a delay
Everyone would have a house and use the door.

If I had a dream
I would be a professional at football
No one would be done
I would never fall
Everyone would always have fun.

If I had a dream
I would be a better friend
No one would ever be in a mood
I would be able to bend
Everyone would have food.

Brendan Cawley (13)
Summerseat Residential School, Bury

My Dream

M ountain bike around Australia
Y acht around the Pacific Ocean

D rive a Ferrari round Brands Hatch
R ow a gondola round Venice
E at at a nice restaurant with Wayne Rooney
A bseil down Mont Blanc
M eet Samuel L Jackson.

Matthew Luttrell (14)
Summerseat Residential School, Bury

I Have A Dream . . .

I have a dream . . .
That people of all races and religions
Would be treated as one.

I have a dream . . .
That people should love
And also respect each other.

I have a dream . . .
That when my children grow up
They should live in a happier and a safe world.

I have a dream . . .
That all people in Africa
Will have food and lots of water.

I have a dream . . .
That people in Africa
Would one day get rid of AIDS for good.

Gerry Conneely (15)
Summerseat Residential School, Bury

My Dream Is . . .

M eet Kyle Minogue
Y ell, when England win the World Cup

D o a job and be successful
R ich, but not famous
E njoy being a mechanic, own a garage
A lways be healthy and happy
M aster of myself

I magine being able to
S ee the whole world.

Ryan Harrison (13)
Summerseat Residential School, Bury

I Have A Dream

A crosser track built for me
I dream the government decide to build crosser tracks
                                    all over the country
To help us stay out of trouble
Young people everywhere cheer at this great news.

The crosser track with its jumps and ramps
Reaching to the sky
Where we can back flip through the air
Like a dolphin in the sea.

Young people from all around
Will meet up to see you can do the best trick
Crosser bikes, the 125 with its gleaming frame so strong
And its wheels so proud
As it speeds through the air like the speed of sound.

I have a dream
A crosser track built for me.

Adam Cooper (15)
Summerseat Residential School, Bury

My Dream

M y dream is to play for Manchester United
Y ou'll see me in my shining boots

D uring my life, I'll be a hero
R emember my name
E very time I get paid, I'll buy a car
A lways fast and
M otorbikes.

Reece Bell (13)
Summerseat Residential School, Bury

Dream

D reams are good
R ules are not in them
E xciting ones
A mazing ones
M emories, everyone has them.

Luke Percival (14)
Summerseat Residential School, Bury

I Have A Dream Of Christmas

I have a dream of Christmas,
It comes every single day,
The presents never-ending
And the tree is here to stay.

The seasons are forgotten,
As it's snowy all year round,
The carol singers smiling,
As they make their festive sound.

The turkey has turned golden
And is made the centre piece,
Crispy bacon at the side -
It's a magic Christmas feast.

But Santa's getting tired
And his reindeer just can't cope,
The elves' jaws hurt from smiling -
They are running out of hope.

So now at last I realise,
As I'm starting to get tired,
Christmas isn't all that good
And Santa might get fired.

Alex Steeland (14)
Upton-by-Chester High School, Chester

Steven Gerrard's Dream

I have a dream
On the pitch
Tired as anything
Thirty-five yards from the goal
Everyone in front
Except my team's defenders
The ball roaring towards me,
'Go on, you can do it,'
My brain said to me in belief
It's my chance
All my power onto the volley
Wow!
Past every player
I send the ball
Straight in the back of the net
This is my dream
And it came true on the 13th May,
In a game against West Ham!

Katie Greenwood (11)
Upton-by-Chester High School, Chester

Who Am I?

Who am I?
Sometimes I am a hero
Saving the world
And other times I am a villain
Causing havoc

Also I can fly
As high as high can get
And other times I have super speed
Running around the world

But then I wake up and wonder
Who I am.

James Kellacher (12)
Upton-by-Chester High School, Chester

I Have A Dream

I live here
In this dreadful world
Of pain and suffering
With nothing else
But myself
Only comrades on the ground
Crying in pain
There's nothing I can do
But carry on
In this war . . . I stand alone
I have a dream
Of relaxation
And food, drinks all around
With my comrades
Having fun
But instead
I lay here
On the ground.

Adam Bradley (12)
Upton-by-Chester High School, Chester

Dreams

Sitting down,
Bored stiff,
Thinking of possibilities,
Dreams,
Daydreams,
How many words can explain it?
Dreaming,
Just dreaming,
To dream about what?
What dream would excite me?
What dream would upset me?
Dreams . . .
Amazing things dreams.

Cara Bebbington (12)
Upton-by-Chester High School, Chester

I Have A Dream
(That Won't Come True)

I have a dream
That won't come true
That my grandad, Eric
Will come alive
My mum says
That he was nice
But I will never know that
Because I wasn't alive
My nan now lives on her own
Now that my grandad has gone
Every time my birthday comes
Guess what I wish for?
I dream that my grandad
Will come alive
Eric Lewis
Dad and husband
And will always be
Remembered.

Charlotte Jones (12)
Upton-by-Chester High School, Chester

Help The Injured - Cure The Ill

I have a dream to be a doctor,
Help the injured and cure the ill,
To appreciate life and how it flies by,
Vaccinate the poorly against disease,
Taking X-rays, hearing people's hearts,
Emotions run through me, as people die.

I have a dream to work in a theatre,
Not singing or dancing, but operating,
Every second counts as the clock ticks on,
Knowing I'm the one who'll save the life,
Whether they live or die, I'll be proud I did my best,
That's my dream and on it will go on.

Sarah Howard (14)
Upton-by-Chester High School, Chester

I Have A Dream

When the sun comes out I scuttle upstairs
And curl up in my nest,
Take a nibble, close my eyes
And take a long rest,
Dreaming about rolling around
In my yellow, shiny ball,
Crashing into the huge furniture
Makes me feel so small,
Then a large pair of warm, soft hands
Bends down and picks me up,
Opens up the cage, gently places me in
And shuts me up,
Then I hear a slight rattle coming from my cage door,
I quickly crawl over to find vegetables galore,
Carrots, cucumber and broccoli too,
Enough to last me a week, maybe even two,
I stuff them in my pouches
And hold on tight to all the rest
And carry them up into my warm, cosy nest.

Harriet Thatcher (12)
Upton-by-Chester High School, Chester

I Have A Dream - Police Officer

I have a dream to work with all the sirens,
I have a dream to work with all the violence,
I have a dream to wear a black and white uniform,
I have a dream to carry handcuffs in my pocket,
I have a dream to say, 'You're nicked!'
I have a dream to slam down doors,
I have a dream to sit and interview people,
I have a dream to drive in a car with the lights flashing,
I have a dream to lock up criminals if they have done wrong,
I have a dream to become a police officer!

Chelsea Woolley (14)
Upton-by-Chester High School, Chester

Even In My Dreams

Sick in bed my mother cries,
I rush to help
Her pills come out
Zitrine, Berethene and all the rest.

Going to the doctors,
All the way to Worcester
The doctor agrees not to send her away,
She gives her new pills and said these should help.

She's walking around, but not too much,
So now she's in bed
And the pills comes out
But she needs a drink.

So now I run down to the kitchen,
To get a glass of water,
Then rush back up
But then I wake up
To my mother's cry.

John Thompson (14)
Upton-by-Chester High School, Chester

I Have A Dream

I have a dream,
To cure all diseases,
To travel the world,
To talk to all species,
To make world peace,
To find my true love,
To make all happiness never ending,
To think before I speak,
To travel through time,
To discover a new universe,
To help other people,
To sit on the edge of the edge of the world,
I have a dream.

Ceri Grube (14)
Upton-by-Chester High School, Chester

Hollywood Dreams

'I used to live in Hollywood,'
My mum once said to me,
'I was young, successful
And living in the land of the brave and the free.'
I wished she would shut up and get back to cooking.

'They wanted to make me a Barbie doll,
Putting me under the knife,
I didn't want to change who I was,
But I wanted a famous life.'
I started to listen properly now.

'It was then I met your father,
I was sheltering from the rain,
He came over and soon we were in love,
In this crazy world, he kept me sane.'
My brother and I made retching noises.

'He begged me to run away with him . . .
I didn't beg, I asked!'
My father was here now, looking indignant,
As if how dare she bring up the past,
'I'm sick of you changing what I say,'
She yelled with much disgust,
'All I wanted was a relationship,
Built on love and trust!'
He left and my mother turned on us.

'Well, that was the end of my stardom,'
She snarled, her eyes alight,
'I gave it all up to be stuck with you kids,
For the rest of my worthless life!'
My brother and I sat gobsmacked,
As she, too, stormed out.

Frances Grindley (14)
Upton-by-Chester High School, Chester

Imagine

Imagine risking it all in a glance
Thinking it would be effortless, like a petal falling to the ground.
Imagine being left breathless
By those three whispered words that bring you closer.
Imagine wanting to spend the rest of your life by his side
And it feeling like the first time, every time.
Imagine being stuck in a moment
That wasn't meant to last
And not wanting to know why you can't stay forever that way.
Imagine every smile
Every letter, every kiss he gave to you.
Imagine letting your heart decide
And getting in too deep.
Imagine nothing comparing to him
Imagine thinking the signs are clear and colourful
Only to realise you have been set up for disappointment.
Imagine it feeling like
You're the last thing on his mind, you can't let go because you're part
of him.
Imagine waiting for the lie to come true
Those lies dropping like acid rain.
Imagine swimming in an ocean all alone
And knowing you have to give up.
It's all so dark and mysterious when the one you want, doesn't want
you.
Imagine your pride being spilt on the floor
His hands and knees are bruised, he'll come crawling back to you.
Love
Is it healing?
Or
Painful?

Natasha Price (15)
Upton-by-Chester High School, Chester

Premonition

I'm walking on a roof up high
There's nothing up here but the sky
I see a face
I slow my pace
She beckons me across.

I walk towards the building's ledge
I take a step right off the edge
I look up see her leaving
Know she's been deceiving
For me she will feel no loss.

I wake before I hit the floor
It's just that dream I've had before
It's my recurring hell each night
Today I'll finally see the light
Today I find out my fate.

I see her from across of town
I walk over and see her frown
I ask her out, she laughs at me
I look at her and finally see
My love for her returned as hate.

Seven nights of solid dreaming
I finally figure out its meaning
Find a razor, cut each vein
Lie down, embrace the pain
My vision blacks, I won't be found.

On a roof I look to the east
My beauty's turned into a beast
I throw myself into open air
The wind rushes through my hair
This time I hit the ground.

Luke Cowieson (14)
Upton-by-Chester High School, Chester

I Have A Dream - Tony Blair's Dream

I step out of the car,
People gasp and take pictures,
Blinding lights,
I step onto the stand.

The crowd falls to silence,
All eyes on me,
My mind filled with ideas,
Ideas to make the world a better place.

They watch in admiration,
Applauding and cheering at every word I say.

Then I'm whisked off,
Surrounded by bodyguards,
Inside a building and into a room,
Filled with news reporters,
Eager,
Eager to ask me questions.

'Will you step down as Prime Minister at the next election?'
What do I say?
The crowd is silent,
Waiting for me to answer.

I dream,
Dream about retirement,
A nice cottage in the countryside,
No stress,
No hassle
And time for my family,
The ones I love the most.

I open my mouth,
Take a gasp
And I wake up.

Rebecca Brierley (15)
Upton-by-Chester High School, Chester

I Have A Dream

I close my eyes
Tightly shut
And imagine being away from this place
A place
Where shouting numbs my ears
Where abuse is said as calmly as a compliment
Where judging eyes follow your every move
And those judging eyes condemn
Where patronising questions are always asked
And the answers are never quite clear
But then again
Vicious words are the norm
For some this place is a living Hell
But I have a dream
That this place is filled with smiles
Where vicious words
And judging eyes
Become a distant myth
I open my eyes
Take a look around
And then I walk to my next lesson.

Ceri Jones (14)
Upton-by-Chester High School, Chester

Haunting You In Your Sleep

I have a dream
Of
Haunting you in your sleep
Making you weak
As the hairs on your back creep
Silently and swiftly
I drift across your room
You hear moans like a breath of death
Echoes in the distance
Death is at your door
For as it's coming closer
You hear it more and more
Evil souls swirl around you
The dead are awakening
To get you
Maybe it's just a dream
But nothing is what it seems
Your heart is pounding
Like the footsteps
With the creaking of your door
Don't make a sound
I'm right there
So don't turn around!

Samantha Carter (15)
Upton-by-Chester High School, Chester

I Have A Dream

I have a dream . . .
Wishing that I could fly like an eagle.
I have a dream . . .
Wishing that I was a snake slithering across the Sahara.
I have a dream . . .
Wishing that all my friends would smile all day.
I have a dream . . .
Wishing I was the Prime Minister.
I have a dream . . .
Wishing I could live in a bubble and no one can pop it.
I have a dream . . .
Wishing I could daydream in all my lessons and the teachers can't
stop me.

I have a dream . . .
Wishing I could walk across the South Arctic.
I have a dream . . .
Wishing I was Ellen MacArthur sailing the Atlantic.
I have a dream . . .
Wishing that I lived in a world where happiness never ended.
I have a dream.

Matthew Owen (14)
Upton-by-Chester High School, Chester

I Had A Dream

A dream of happiness,
But I know that it would not happen,
I have seen too much sadness,
Too much anguish in my life,
I can't just forget it and move on,
I can't forget what has happened,
I can't erase it from my memory,
I had a dream.

Rachael Langan (14)
Upton-by-Chester High School, Chester

I Have A Dream

Swimming around in the cool, calm water,
As my tail flips up, it shimmers in the sun,
My gills fill up with fresh sea water
And then beautiful bubbles escape from my mouth.
Suddenly they burst with a terrifying pop
Giving the ocean a frightful shock.
A black swirling whirlpool surrounds me, pulling down
To the depths of the sea.
Rocks tumble down and slimy seaweed tangles around me
Snatching me to safety,
As the rocks crash down, to the sandy seabed
The slippery arms slide away,
I start to shiver as the water turns cold,
Quietness surrounds me,
Everything seems to have stopped moving.
I try to flap my fins, fill up my gills and blow a bubble,
It isn't happening
There's no water
Everything has frozen,
Trapping me in ice,
My life fades away before me,
As I try to take my last breath
I realise it's the end,
There's nothing else I can do.
But then, with a sudden crack and a trickle of water,
My bad dream has disappeared
And I'm safe and sound, swimming around in the cool, calm water.
What's happening to me?
I've forgotten!

Miriam Peers (12)
Upton-by-Chester High School, Chester

I Have A Dream . . .

I have a dream . . .
That I could help the world.
I have a dream . . .
To stop world hunger.
I have a dream . . .
To save the environment.
I have a dream . . .
To stop animal abuse.
I have a dream . . .
To care for the sick.
I have a dream,
To make the world happy.
I have a dream,
That peace can be had.
I have a dream . . .
That all these dreams come true.
I have a dream . . .
And it all depends on *you!*

Jenny Hughes (13)
Upton-by-Chester High School, Chester

Dreams Of The Hopeful

No more suffering
No more pain
That's what I dream of
No more crying
No more loss
That's what I dream of
No more bombings
No more death
That's what I dream of.

Lots of joy
Lots of hope
That's what I dream of
Lots of health
Lots of love
That's what I dream of
Life is for living
Dreams are for dreaming
That's why I dream.

Sophie Wilding (15)
Upton-by-Chester High School, Chester

I Have A Dream - Peace At Last

I have a dream
Where suffering is no more
The world lives in harmony
But the memories are still sore

People remember
When the world was torn apart
By raging wars and famine
Arguing over money, what a pointless start

But soon they all thought
How pointless war really was
Innocent lives lost forever
Damaging all of us

So war is over
All the people are rejoicing
The world is at peace at last
And I will keep dreaming.

Nia Edwards (15)
Upton-by-Chester High School, Chester

English Target

I have a dream
To write well
I want to show the world
That you may be rubbish
At it but work hard
And you will do well
I am not the best at English
But I keep at it
I have a dream
To publish books
To write about dragons
And warriors
To create an amazing
World of my own
And be known
All over the world

I have a dream.

Hannah Perry (12)
Upton-by-Chester High School, Chester

I Have A Dream

As the clock ticks on,
The world spins round,
Everyone in their own lives,
Forever wishing,
Forever dreaming,
Wars to end,
Peace to reign.

For all the people to dream one dream,
For the world to be calm,
For violence to come to an end,
For bullies to rethink their actions,
For people's lives to be content,
This is my dream and if I had the power, I would change it all.

But the pendulum swings on
And so do my dreams,
The world turns,
The coin spins,
The dice rolls,
What side will it land on?
No one knows,
But if I had my dream, I'd change it all.

Ellen Craig (14)
Upton-by-Chester High School, Chester

I Have A Dream

I have a dream
That my grey hair is blonde again,
My poor eyesight is sharp once more,
My withered skin is smooth as silk,
I am young again.

I am a girl,
Dancing through the fields of daisies,
Going towards my family's house.
Honeysuckle creeps up the wall,
It's a perfect home.

I go inside,
Where my family is gathered,
Around the great wooden table.
Ma and Pa, sisters and brothers
Are waiting for me.

Then he walks in,
Smiling and laughing, he joins me.
Young and handsome and big and strong,
When he put his arms around me,
My heart fills with love.

So when I dream
I am with the people I love
And lost over the long, long years.
I'm young and strong, happy and loved
And so I dream on.

Stephanie Kelly (15)
Upton-by-Chester High School, Chester

Ace The Astronaut

I am a goldfish, my name is Ace,
But I have a dream where I blast into space,
I want to witness life outside my bowl,
I want to be an astronaut before I grow old.

I don't want to be a musician or drive a fast car,
Just to admire the Earth from afar,
I don't crave publicity or wish to be famous,
All I really want is to gaze upon Uranus.

I'd have a special water-filled ship,
Built for me by my cousin Rick,
It would keep me safe day and night,
As I zoom around at the speed of light.

But I fear my existence is as hollow as my castle,
I think I'll save myself all the hassle,
I won't attempt to see the stars,
I'll stay down here with my pet tadpole, Lars.

Karis Vaughan (15)
Upton-by-Chester High School, Chester

Imagine

Imagine your feelings
And if you could change them would the world be a better place?
Imagine your fears
And if you were loved or not loved in return
Imagine suffering
And if you could, would you save people the pain?
Imagine life
And if you could start again, would you?
Imagine sunset
And if it meant the end of the best day of your life.

What do you do when the ability to imagine has left you?
What do you say when fantasies are no more?
What do you do when love seems to give up
And how can life be so hard, you feel like giving up?
But always remember after a sunset, there is always a sunrise.

Rebecca Addison (15)
Upton-by-Chester High School, Chester

Changing The World

The world is not a perfect place,
People spit and cough in your face,
Violence and racism should be banned,
Everyone give a helping hand.

The word war should have no meaning,
It would be so perfect,
Poverty, no longer exists,
It would just be great.

Swearing made an utter disgrace,
No favouritism to different race,
All things should be fair,
Everyone has time to spare.

Peter Pegasiou (12)
Wirral Grammar School for Boys, Wirral

I Had A Dream

I had a dream
That there was no war
Everything was peaceful
And no one was poor

There was no more death
And no more hurt
There was no more sadness
In the entire world

If this wasn't a dream
And everything was real
We could live a happy life
And we wouldn't live in fear

But none of this will happen
Unless we see some change
Which will help this world get better
And make it a nicer place.

Andrew McEwan (12)
Wirral Grammar School for Boys, Wirral

I Had A Dream

I had a dream,
That the world was a better place,
No poverty, war or hunger,
Just peace and prosperity.

Few dreams come true
And few wishes are granted,
But I hope one thing,
That this dream will come true.

Everyone has dreams,
But all of them are different,
As I said, my dream would be,
Throughout the world, peace and prosperity.

No fighting, no guns,
No starving or dying,
No poverty or greed,
Just a fair share of everything!

Daniel Galvin (12)
Wirral Grammar School for Boys, Wirral

I Have A Dream . . .

I have a dream . . .
A dream of the world in unity
A dream of the world in peace
A dream of the world in stability.

I have a dream . . .
A dream of brotherhood
A dream of racial equality
A dream of true friendship.

I have a dream . . .
A dream of freedom
A dream of happiness
A dream of faith.

I have a dream . . .
A dream of hope
A dream of new things
And new life.

But most of all,
I have a dream . . .
Of new beginnings.

William Ekuban (12)
Wirral Grammar School for Boys, Wirral

I Have A Dream

My dream is simple
To live in peace
No more fighting
No more grief

My dream is simple
To feel secure
No more torture
No more war

My dream is simple
To live without fear
No more torment
No more tears

My dream is simple
To have all our needs
No more poverty
No more greed

My dream seems simple
But that's far from true
Many are suffering
What about you?

James Lewis (12)
Wirral Grammar School for Boys, Wirral

I Have A Dream . . .

I have a dream . . .
The terror was over,
I have a dream . . .
The cliffs were still white at Dover.

I have a dream . . .
That all hurt was gone,
I have a dream . . .
That evil touched no one.

I have a dream . . .
That peace was ever-lasting,
I have a dream . . .
That there was no need for nuclear blasting.

I have a dream . . .
But to make this dream come true
I will need the dreams
Of every one of you.

Matthew Brennan (12)
Wirral Grammar School for Boys, Wirral